BLACK&DECKER®
HOME IMPROVEMENT LIBRARY™

Home Plumbing Projects & Repairs

Cy DeCosse Incorporated
Minnetonka, Minnesota

Contents

Copyright © 1990
Cy DeCosse Incorporated
5900 Green Oak Drive
Minnetonka, Minnesota 55343
1-800-328-3895
All rights reserved
Printed in Mexico

Also available from the publisher:
*Everyday Home Repairs, Decorating With
Paint & Wallcovering, Carpentry: Tools •
Shelves • Walls • Doors, Kitchen
Remodeling, Building Decks, Basic Wiring
& Electrical Repairs, Workshop Tips &
Techniques, Advanced Home Wiring,
Carpentry: Remodeling, Landscape
Design & Construction, Bathroom
Remodeling*

Library of Congress
Cataloging-in-Publication Data

Home plumbing projects & repairs.

p. cm. — (Black & Decker home
improvement library)
ISBN 0-86573-710-X
ISBN 0-86573-711-8 (pbk.)
1. Plumbing - Amateurs' manuals
2. Plumbing — Repairing — Amateurs'
manuals.
I. Cy DeCosse Incorporated II. Title: Home
plumbing projects & repairs. III. Series.
TH6124.H613 1990   90-32979
696'.1 — dc20   CIP

CY DECOSSE INCORPORATED
Chairman: Cy DeCosse
President: James B. Maus
Executive Vice President: William B. Jones

Created by: The Editors of Cy DeCosse
Incorporated, in cooperation with Black &
Decker. **BLACK&DECKER** is a trademark of
the Black & Decker Corporation, and is
used under license.

Toilets & Drains

Tubs & Showers

Water Heaters

Emergency Repairs

Project Director: John Riha
Project Manager: Dianne Talmage
Senior Art Director: Tim Himsel
Art Director: Dave Schelitzche
Editor: Bryan Trandem
Technical Production Editor: Paul Currie
Copy Editors: Janice Cauley, Bernice
  Maehren
Production Director: Jim Bindas
Production Manager: Amelia Merz
Production Art Supervisor: Julie Churchill

Shop Supervisor: Greg Wallace
Prop Stylist: Jim Huntley

Production Staff: Joe Fahey, Kevin D. Frakes,
  Melissa Grabanski, Mark Jacobson,
  Yelena Konrardy, Daniel Meyers, Linda
  Schloegel, Nik Wogstad

Director of Photography: Tony Kubat
Studio Manager: Cathleen Shannon
Assistant Studio Manager: Rebecca DaWald

Photographers: Phil Aarrestad, Kim Baily,
  Paul Englund, Rex Irmen, John Lauenstein,
  Bill Lindner, Mark Macemon, Charles
  Nields, Mette Nielsen, Cathleen Shannon

Contributing Editor: Merle Henkenius
Contributing Manufacturers: Cooper
  Industries; The Irwin Company; Price
  Pfister; Waxman Industries, Inc.

Printer: R. R. Donnelley & Sons Co. (0194)

Introduction

Plumbing problems are a fact of life for any homeowner. Over time, faucets develop leaks, clogs block drain lines, and appliances wear out and need to be replaced. As a homeowner, you can either call a professional plumber, or save hundreds of dollars by making your own repairs.

Home Plumbing Projects & Repairs is a complete repair manual designed to guide homeowners through virtually any plumbing repair project. With expert advice from professional plumbers and hundreds of detailed, step-by-step color photographs, *Home Plumbing Projects & Repairs* ensures your success.

To help you gain an understanding of how plumbing works, the opening pages give you a dramatic look at an entire home plumbing system, with all pipes color-coded for easy identification. Included are detailed descriptions of each part of the plumbing system to help you diagnose problems and plan possible repairs.

Next, a catalog of tools helps you identify the common hand tools, specialty plumbing tools, power tools, and rental tools that are used in this book. Use this section to quickly identify tools that may be necessary to complete your repairs.

A section on materials is one of the most useful portions of this book. Not only will you learn about the many different kinds of pipes and fittings available, but also how to cut, fit, repair, and replace each kind. Because we cannot anticipate all your working conditions or the configuration of your plumbing system, this overview will give you the knowledge and skills necessary to complete any repair or replacement project.

The majority of this book is devoted to fixing the wide variety of plumbing problems that may occur in the typical home. A section on faucet repair is one of the most complete and easy-to-understand faucet repair guidelines ever published. In addition, you'll learn how to fix and maintain toilets, all types of drains, tub and shower plumbing, and both electric and gas water heaters. You'll discover dozens of professional tips to make each job easier and faster, as well as complete information on how to remove and replace faucets, toilets, and water heaters.

A final section provides information on how to prevent or repair some of the most common plumbing annoyances: burst, frozen, or noisy pipes.

We're proud to offer this solid, comprehensive reference book, and we're confident *Home Plumbing Projects & Repairs* will be an important addition to your home library.

NOTICE TO READERS

This book provides useful instructions, but we cannot anticipate all of your working conditions or the characteristics of your materials and tools. For safety, you should use caution, care, and good judgment when following the procedures described in this book. Consider your own skill level and the instructions and safety precautions associated with the various tools and materials shown. Neither the publisher nor Black & Decker® can assume responsibility for any damage to property or injury to persons as a result of the misuse of the information provided.

The instructions in this book conform to "The Uniform Plumbing Code," "The National Electrical Code Reference Book," and "The Uniform Building Code" current at the time of its original publication. Consult your local Building Department for information on building permits, codes, and other laws as they apply to your project.

The Home Plumbing System

Because most of a plumbing system is hidden inside walls and floors, it may seem to be a complex maze of pipes and fittings. In fact, home plumbing is simple and straightforward. Understanding how home plumbing works is an important first step toward doing routine maintenance and money-saving repairs.

A typical home plumbing system includes three basic parts: a water supply system, fixtures and appliances, and a drain system. These three parts can be seen clearly in the photograph of the cutaway house on the opposite page.

Fresh water enters a home through a main supply line (1). This fresh water source is provided by either a municipal water company or a private underground well. If the source is a municipal supplier, the water passes through a meter (2) that registers the amount of water used. A family of four uses about four hundred gallons of water each day.

Immediately after the main supply enters the house, a branch line splits off (3) and is joined to a hot water heater (4). From the water heater, a hot water line runs parallel to the cold water line to bring the water supply to fixtures and appliances throughout the house. Fixtures include sinks, bathtubs, showers, and laundry tubs. Appliances include water heaters, dishwashers, clothes washers, and water softeners. Toilets and exterior sillcocks are examples of fixtures that require only a cold water line.

The water supply to fixtures and appliances is controlled with faucets and valves. Faucets and valves have moving parts and seals that eventually may wear out or break, but they are easily repaired or replaced.

Waste water then enters the drain system. It first must flow past a trap (5), a U-shaped piece of pipe that holds standing water and prevents sewer gases from entering the home. Every fixture must have a drain trap.

The drain system works entirely by gravity, allowing waste water to flow downhill through a series of large-diameter pipes. These drain pipes are attached to a system of vent pipes. Vent pipes (6) bring fresh air to the drain system, preventing suction that would slow or stop drain water from flowing freely. Vent pipes usually exit the house at a roof vent (7).

All waste water eventually reaches a main waste and vent stack (8). The main stack curves to become a sewer line (9) that exits the house near the foundation. In a municipal system, this sewer line joins a main sewer line located near the street. Where sewer service is not available, waste water empties into a septic system.

Water meter and main shutoff valve are located where the main water supply pipe enters the house. The water meter is the property of your local municipal water company. If the water meter leaks, or if you suspect it is not functioning properly, call your water company for repairs.

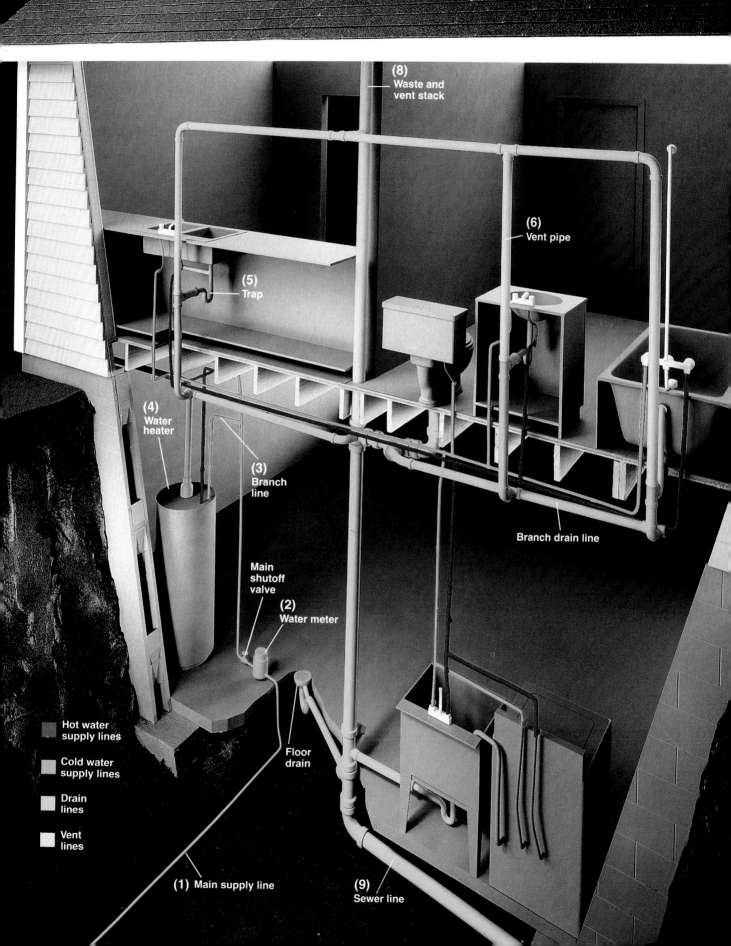

(7) Roof vent

(8) Waste and vent stack

(6) Vent pipe

(5) Trap

(4) Water heater

(3) Branch line

Main shutoff valve

(2) Water meter

Branch drain line

Floor drain

Hot water supply lines

Cold water supply lines

Drain lines

Vent lines

(1) Main supply line

(9) Sewer line

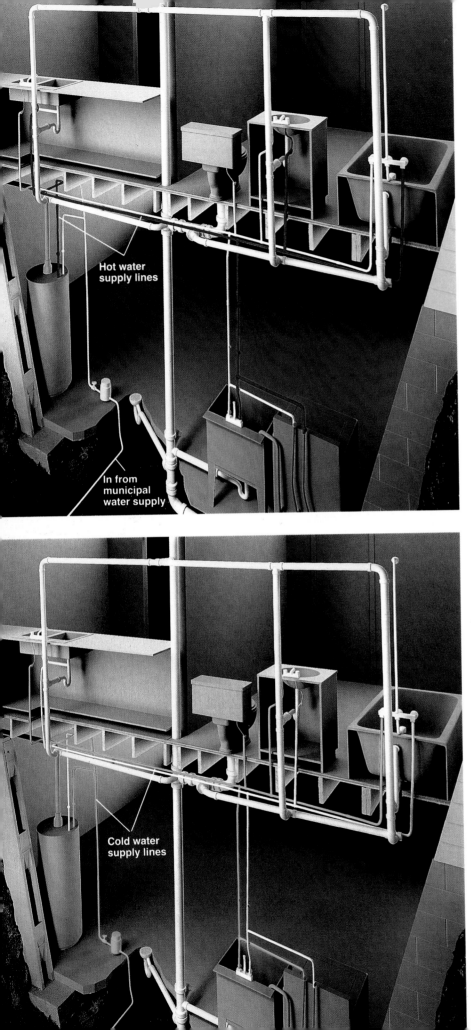

Hot water
supply lines

In from
municipal
water supply

Cold water
supply lines

Water Supply System

Water supply pipes carry hot and cold water throughout a house. In homes built before 1950, the original supply pipes are usually made of galvanized iron. Newer homes have supply pipes made of copper. In some areas of the country, supply pipes made of plastic are gaining acceptance by local plumbing codes.

Water supply pipes are made to withstand the high pressures of the water supply system. They have small diameters, usually ½" to 1", and are joined with strong, watertight fittings. The hot and cold lines run in tandem to all parts of the house. Usually, the supply pipes run inside wall cavities or are strapped to the undersides of floor joists.

Hot and cold water supply pipes are connected to fixtures or appliances. Fixtures include sinks, tubs, and showers. Some fixtures, such as toilets or hose bibs, are supplied only by cold water. Appliances include dishwashers and clothes washers. A refrigerator is an example of an appliance that uses only cold water. Tradition says that hot water supply pipes and faucet handles are found on the left-hand side of a fixture. Cold water is on the right.

Because of high water pressure, leaks are the most common problems for the water supply system. This is especially true of galvanized iron pipe, which has limited resistance to corrosion.

Drain, Waste, Vent System

Drain pipes use gravity to carry waste water away from fixtures, appliances, and other drains. This waste water is carried out of the house to a municipal sewer system or septic tank.

Drain pipes are usually plastic or cast iron. In some older homes, drain pipes may be made of copper or lead. Because they are not part of the supply system, lead drain pipes pose no health hazard. However, lead pipes are no longer manufactured for home plumbing systems.

Drain pipes have diameters ranging from 1¼" to 4". These large diameters allow waste water to pass easily.

Traps are an important part of the drain system. These curved sections of drain pipe hold standing water, and they are usually found near any drain opening. The standing water of a trap prevents sewer gases from backing up into the home. Each time a drain is used, the standing trap water is flushed away and is replaced by new water.

In order to work properly, the drain system requires air. Air allows waste water to flow freely down drain pipes.

To allow air into the drain system, drain pipes are connected to vent pipes. All drain systems must include vents, and the entire system is called the drain, waste, vent (DWV) system. One or more vent stacks, located on the roof, provide the air needed for the DWV system to work.

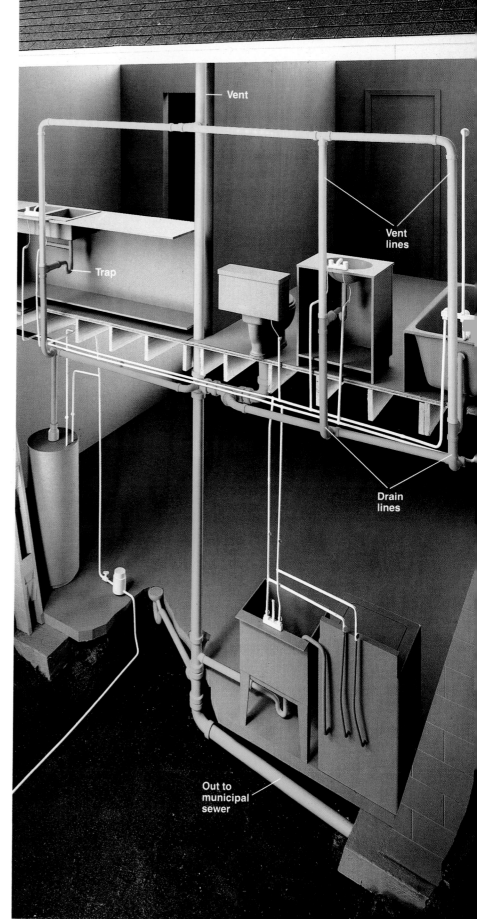

Vent

Vent lines

Trap

Drain lines

Out to municipal sewer

Tools for Plumbing

Many plumbing projects and repairs can be completed with basic hand tools you probably already own. Adding a few simple plumbing tools will prepare you for all the projects in this book. Specialty tools, such as a cast iron cutter or appliance dolly, are available at rental centers. When buying tools, invest in quality products.

Always care for tools properly. Clean tools after using them, wiping them free of dirt and dust with a soft rag. Prevent rust on metal tools by wiping them with a rag dipped in household oil. If a metal tool gets wet, dry it immediately, and then wipe it with an oiled rag. Keep tool boxes and cabinets organized. Make sure all tools are stored securely.

Caulk gun is designed to hold tubes of caulk or glue. A squeeze handle pushes a steady bead of caulk or glue out of the nozzle.

Flashlight is an indispensable plumber's helper for inspecting pipes and drain openings.

Circuit tester is an important safety device that allows the user to test for live current in an electrical outlet or appliance. Also referred to as *testing for hot wires*.

Ratchet wrench is used for tightening or loosening bolts and nuts. It has interchangeable sockets for adapting to different sized bolts or nuts.

Hacksaw is used for cutting metals. Also can be used for cutting plastic pipes. Has replaceable blades.

Small wire brush has soft brass bristles for cleaning metals without damaging surfaces.

Utility knife has a razor-sharp blade for cutting a wide variety of materials. Useful for trimming ends of plastic pipes. For safety, the utility knife should have a retractable blade.

Cold chisel is used with a *ball peen hammer* to cut or chip ceramic tile, mortar, or hardened metals.

Files are used to smooth the edges of metal, wood, or plastic. The *round file* (top) can be used to remove burrs from the insides of pipes. The *flat file* is used for all general smoothing tasks.

Ball peen hammer is made for striking metallic objects, like a *cold chisel*. The head of a ball peen hammer is made to resist chipping.

Screwdrivers include the two most common types: the *slotted* (top), and the *phillips*.

Adjustable wrench has a movable jaw that permits the wrench to fit a wide variety of bolt heads or nuts.

Channel-type pliers has a movable handle that allows the jaws to be adjusted for maximum gripping strength. The insides of the jaws are serrated to prevent slipping.

Wooden mallet is used for striking nonmetallic objects, such as plastic drywall anchors.

Needlenose pliers has thin jaws for gripping small objects, or for reaching into confined areas.

Putty knife is especially helpful for scraping away old putty or caulk from appliances and fixtures.

Tape measure should have a retractable steel blade at least 16 feet long.

Level is used for setting new appliances and checking the slope of exhaust ducts.

Tubing cutter makes straight, smooth cuts in plastic and copper pipe. A tubing cutter usually has a dull, triangular blade, called a *reaming tip*, for removing burrs from the insides of pipes.

Closet auger is used to clear toilet clogs. It is a slender tube with a crank handle on one end of a flexible auger cable. A special bend in the tube allows the auger to be positioned in the bottom of the toilet bowl. The bend is usually protected with a rubber sleeve to prevent scratching the toilet.

Plastic tubing cutter works like a gardener's pruners to cut flexible plastic (PB) pipes quickly.

Spud wrench is specially designed for removing or tightening large nuts that are 2" to 4" in diameter. Hooks on the ends of the wrench grab onto the *lugs* of large nuts for increased leverage.

Plunger clears drain clogs with water and air pressure. The *flanged plunger* (shown) is used for toilet bowls. The flange usually can be folded up into the cup for use as a *standard plunger*. Use a standard plunger to clear clogs in sink, tub, shower, and floor drains.

Hand auger, sometimes called a *snake*, is used to clear clogs in drain lines. A long, flexible steel cable is stored in the disk-shaped crank. A pistol-grip handle allows the user to apply steady pressure on the cable.

Blow bag, sometimes called an *expansion nozzle*, is used to clear drains. It attaches to a garden hose and removes clogs with powerful spurts of water. The blow bag is best used on floor drains.

Propane torch (left) is used for soldering fittings to copper pipes. Light the torch quickly and safely using a **spark lighter** (above).

Pipe wrench has a movable jaw that adjusts to fit a variety of pipe diameters. Pipe wrench is used for tightening and loosening pipes, pipe fittings, and large nuts. Two pipe wrenches often are used together to prevent damage to pipes and fittings.

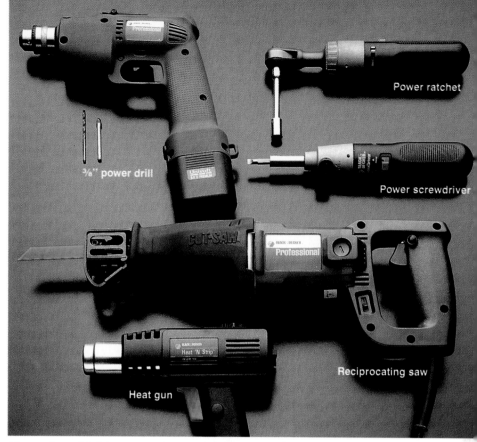

3/8" power drill

Power ratchet

Power screwdriver

Reciprocating saw

Heat gun

Power hand tools can make any job faster, easier, and safer. Cordless power tools offer added convenience. Use a cordless 3/8" **power drill** for virtually any drilling task. A cordless **power ratchet** makes it easy to turn small nuts or hex-head bolts. The cordless reversible **power screwdriver** drives a wide variety of screws and fasteners. A **reciprocating saw** uses interchangeable blades to cut wood, metal, or plastic. Thaw frozen pipes fast with a **heat gun.**

Motorized drain auger

Power miter box

Appliance dolly

Right-angle drill

Cast iron cutter

Rental tools may be needed for large jobs and special situations. A **power miter box** makes fast, accurate cuts in a wide variety of materials, including plastic pipes. A **motorized drain auger** clears tree roots from sewer service lines. Use an **appliance dolly** to move heavy objects like water heaters. A **cast iron cutter** is designed to cut tough cast-iron pipes. The **right-angle drill** is useful for drilling holes in hard-to-reach areas.

Plumbing Materials

Check local plumbing code for materials allowed in your area. All diameters specified are the interior diameters (I.D.) of pipes.

Benefits & Characteristics

Cast iron is very strong, but is difficult to cut and fit. Repairs and replacements should be made with plastic pipe, if allowed by local code.

ABS (Acrylonitrile-Butadiene-Styrene) was the first rigid plastic approved for use in home drain systems. Some local plumbing codes now restrict the use of ABS in new installations.

PVC (Poly-Vinyl-Chloride) is a modern rigid plastic that is highly resistant to damage by heat or chemicals. It is the best material for drain-waste-vent pipes.

Galvanized iron is very strong, but gradually will corrode. Not advised for new installation. Because galvanized iron is difficult to cut and fit, large jobs are best left to a professional.

CPVC (Chlorinated-Poly-Vinyl-Chloride) rigid plastic is chemically formulated to withstand the high temperatures and pressures of water supply systems. Pipes and fittings are inexpensive.

PB (Poly-Butylene) flexible plastic is easy to fit. It bends easily around corners and requires fewer fittings than CPVC. Not all local codes have been updated to permit use of PB pipe.

Rigid copper is the best material for water supply pipes. It resists corrosion, and has smooth surfaces that provide good water flow. Soldered copper joints are very durable.

Chromed copper has an attractive shiny surface, and is used in areas where appearance is important. Chromed copper is durable and easy to bend and fit.

Flexible copper tubing is easy to shape, and will withstand a slight frost without rupturing. Flexible copper bends easily around corners, so it requires fewer fittings than rigid copper.

Brass is heavy and durable. **Chromed brass** has an attractive shiny surface, and is used for drain traps where appearance is important.

Common Uses	Lengths	Diameters	Fitting Methods	Tools Used for Cutting
Main drain-waste-vent pipes	5 ft., 10 ft.	3", 4"	Joined with banded neoprene couplings	Cast iron cutter or hacksaw
Drain & vent pipes; drain traps	10 ft., 20 ft.; or sold by linear ft.	1½", 2", 3", 4"	Joined with solvent glue and plastic fittings	Tubing cutter, miter box, or hacksaw
Drain & vent pipes; drain traps	10 ft., 20 ft.; or sold by linear ft.	1½", 2", 3", 4"	Joined with solvent glue and plastic fittings	Tubing cutter, miter box, or hacksaw
Drains; hot & cold water supply pipes	1" to 1-ft. nipples; custom lengths up to 20 ft.	½", ¾", 1", 1½", 2"	Joined with galvanized threaded fittings	Hacksaw or reciprocating saw
Hot & cold water supply pipes	10 ft.	⅜", ½", ¾", 1"	Joined with solvent glue and plastic fittings, or with grip fittings	Tubing cutter, miter box, or hacksaw
Hot & cold water supply, where allowed by code	25-ft., 100-ft. coils; or sold by linear ft.	⅜", ½", ¾"	Joined with plastic grip fittings	Flexible plastic tubing cutter, sharp knife, or miter box
Hot & cold water supply pipes	10 ft., 20 ft.; or sold by linear ft.	⅜", ½", ¾", 1"	Joined with metal solder or compression fittings	Tubing cutter, hacksaw, or jig saw
Supply tubing for plumbing fixtures	12", 20", 30"	⅜"	Joined with brass compression fittings	Tubing cutter or hacksaw
Gas tubing; hot & cold water supply tubing	30-ft., 60-ft. coils; or sold by linear ft.	¼", ⅜", ½", ¾", 1"	Joined with brass flare fittings, compression fittings, or metal solder	Tubing cutter or hacksaw
Valves & shutoffs; chromed drain traps	Lengths vary	¼", ½", ¾"; *for drain traps:* 1¼", 1½"	Joined with compression fittings, or with metal solder	Tubing cutter, hacksaw, or reciprocating saw

Water Supply Fittings

Copper   Galvanized   CPVC
iron

Drain-Waste-Vent Fittings

ABS   PVC

90° elbows are used to make right-angle bends in a pipe run. Drain-waste-vent (DWV) elbows are curved to prevent debris from being trapped in the bend.

T-fittings are used to connect branch lines in water supply and drain-waste-vent systems. A T-fitting used in a DWV system is called a "waste-T" or "sanitary T."

Couplings are used to join two straight pipes. Special transition fittings (page opposite) are used to join two pipes that are made from different materials.

Reducers connect pipes of different diameters. Reducing T-fittings and elbows are also available.

45° elbows are used to make gradual bends in a pipe run. Elbows are also available with 60° and 72° bends.

Plumbing Fittings

Plumbing fittings come in different shapes to let you form branch lines, change the direction of a pipe run, or connect pipes of different sizes. Transition fittings are used to connect pipes and fixtures that are made from different materials (page opposite). Fittings come in many sizes, but the basic shapes are standard to all metal and plastic pipes. In general, fittings used to connect drain pipes have gradual bends for a smooth flow of drain water.

How to Use Transition Fittings

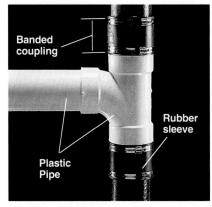

Connect plastic to cast iron with banded couplings (pages 42 to 45). Rubber sleeves cover ends of pipes and ensure a watertight joint.

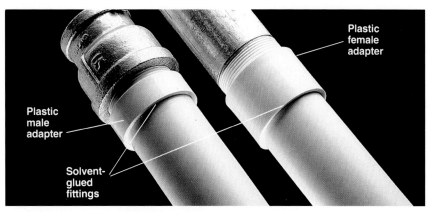

Connect plastic to threaded metal pipes with male and female threaded adapters. Plastic adapter is solvent-glued to plastic pipe. Threads of pipe should be wrapped with Teflon™ tape. Metal pipe is then screwed directly to the adapter.

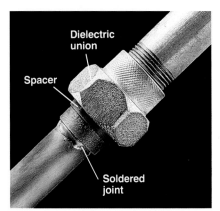

Connect copper to galvanized iron with a dielectric union. Union is threaded onto iron pipe, and is soldered to copper pipe. A dielectric union has plastic spacer that prevents corrosion caused by electrochemical reaction between metals.

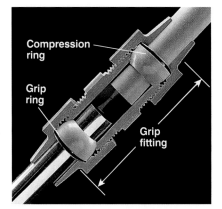

Connect plastic to copper with a grip fitting. Each side of the fitting (shown in cutaway) contains a narrow grip ring and a plastic compression ring (or rubber O-ring) that forms the seal.

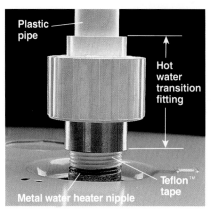

Connect metal hot water pipe to plastic with a hot water transition fitting that prevents leaks caused by different expansion rates of materials. Metal pipe threads are wrapped with Teflon™ tape. Plastic pipe is solvent-glued to fitting.

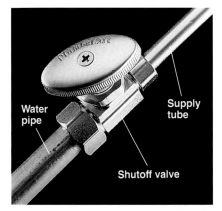

Connect a water pipe to any fixture supply tube, using a shutoff valve (pages 64 to 65).

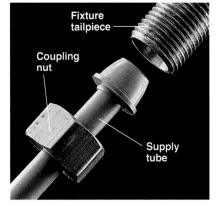

Connect any supply tube to a fixture tailpiece with a coupling nut. Coupling nut seals the bell-shaped end of supply tube against the fixture tailpiece.

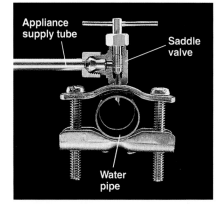

Connect appliance supply tube to copper pipe with a saddle valve (page 69). Saddle valve (shown in cutaway) often is used to connect a refrigerator icemaker.

Working with Copper

Copper is the ideal material for water supply pipes. It resists corrosion and has smooth surfaces that provide good water flow. Copper pipes are available in several diameters (page 15) but most home water supply systems use ½" or ¾" pipe. Copper pipe is manufactured in rigid and flexible forms.

Rigid copper, sometimes called hard copper, is approved for home water supply systems by all local codes. It comes in three wall-thickness grades: Types M, L, and K. Type M is the thinnest, the least expensive, and a good choice for do-it-yourself home plumbing.

Rigid Type L usually is required by codes for commercial plumbing systems. Because it is strong and solders easily, Type L may be preferred by some professional plumbers and do-it-yourselfers for home use. Type K has the heaviest wall thickness, and is used most often for underground water service lines.

Flexible copper, also called soft copper, comes in two wall-thickness grades: Types L and K. Both are approved for most home water supply systems, although flexible Type L copper is used primarily for gas service lines. Because it is bendable and will resist a mild frost, Type L may be installed as part of a water supply system in unheated indoor areas, like crawl spaces. Type K is used for underground water service lines.

A third form of copper, called DWV, is used for drain systems. Because most codes now allow low-cost plastic pipes for drain systems, DWV copper is seldom used.

Copper pipes are connected with soldered, compression, or flare fittings (see chart below). Always follow your local code for the correct types of pipes and fittings allowed in your area.

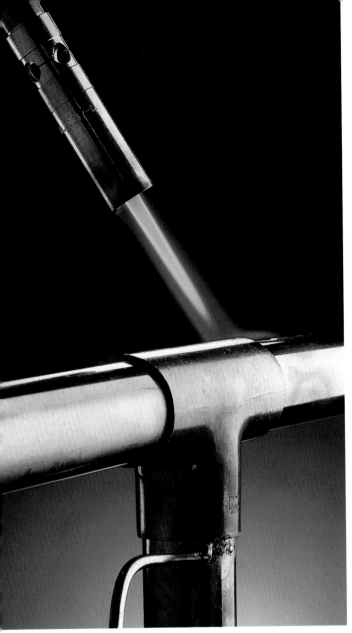

Soldered fittings, also called sweat fittings, often are used to join copper pipes. Correctly soldered fittings (pages 20 to 24), are strong and trouble-free. Copper pipe can also be joined with compression fittings (pages 26 to 27) or flare fittings (pages 28 to 29). See chart below.

Copper Pipe & Fitting Chart

Fitting Method	Rigid Copper			Flexible Copper		General Comments
	Type M	Type L	Type K	Type L	Type K	
Soldered	yes	yes	yes	yes	yes	Inexpensive, strong, and trouble-free fitting method. Requires some skill.
Compression	yes	not recommended		yes	yes	Easy to use. Allows pipes or fixtures to be repaired or replaced readily. More expensive than solder. Best used on flexible copper.
Flare	no	no	no	yes	yes	Use only with flexible copper pipes. Usually used as a gas-line fitting. Requires some skill.

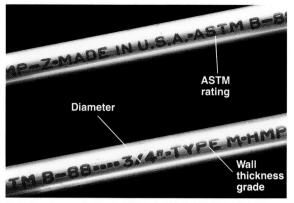

Grade stamp information includes pipe diameter, the wall-thickness grade, and a stamp of approval from the ASTM (American Society for Testing and Materials). Type M pipe is identified by red lettering, Type L by blue lettering.

Bend flexible copper pipe with a coil-spring tubing bender to avoid kinks. Select a bender that matches the outside diameter of the pipe. Slip bender over pipe using a twisting motion. Bend pipe slowly until it reaches the correct angle, but not more than 90°.

Specialty tools & materials for working with copper include: flaring tool (A), emery cloth (B), coil-spring tubing bender (C), pipe joint compound (D), self-cleaning soldering paste (flux) (E), lead-free solder (F), wire brush (G), flux brush (H), compression fitting (I), flare fitting (J).

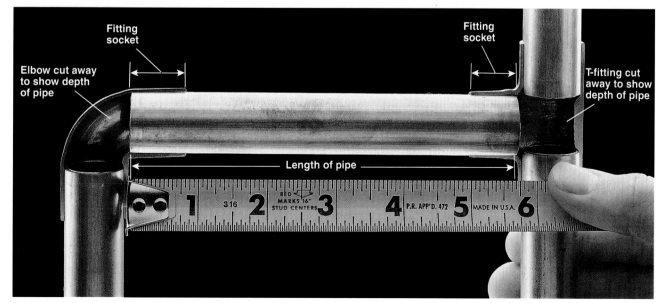

Find length of copper pipe needed by measuring between the bottom of the copper fitting sockets (fittings shown in cutaway). Mark length on the pipe with a felt-tipped pen.

Cutting & Soldering Copper

The best way to cut rigid and flexible copper pipe is with a tubing cutter. A tubing cutter makes a smooth, straight cut, an important first step toward making a watertight joint. Remove any metal burrs on the cut edges with a reaming tool or round file.

Copper can be cut with a hacksaw. A hacksaw is useful in tight areas where a tubing cutter will not fit. Take care to make a smooth, straight cut when cutting with a hacksaw.

A soldered pipe joint, also called a sweated joint, is made by heating a copper or brass fitting with a propane torch until the fitting is just hot enough to melt metal solder. The heat draws the solder into the gap between the fitting and pipe to form a watertight seal. A fitting that is overheated or unevenly heated will not draw in solder. Copper pipes and fittings must be clean and dry to form a watertight seal.

Everything You Need:

Tools: tubing cutter with reaming tip (or hacksaw and round file), wire brush, flux brush, propane torch, spark lighter (or matches), adjustable wrench, channel-type pliers.

Materials: copper pipe, copper fittings, emery cloth, soldering paste (flux), sheet metal, lead-free solder, rag.

Protect wood from heat of the torch flame while soldering, using a double layer (two 18" × 18" pieces) of 26-gauge sheet metal. Buy sheet metal at hardware stores or building supply centers, and keep it to use with all soldering projects.

Soldering Tips

Use caution when soldering copper. Pipes and fittings become very hot and must be allowed to cool before handling.

Keep joint dry when soldering existing water pipes by plugging the pipe with bread. Bread absorbs moisture that may ruin the soldering process and cause pinhole leaks. The bread dissolves when water is turned back on.

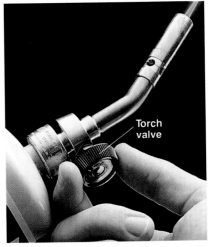

Torch valve

Prevent accidents by shutting off propane torch immediately after use. Make sure valve is closed completely.

How to Cut Rigid & Flexible Copper Pipe

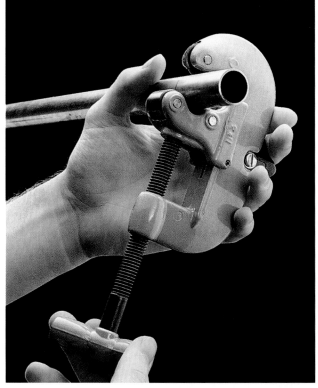

1 Place tubing cutter over the pipe and tighten the handle so that pipe rests on both rollers, and cutting wheel is on marked line.

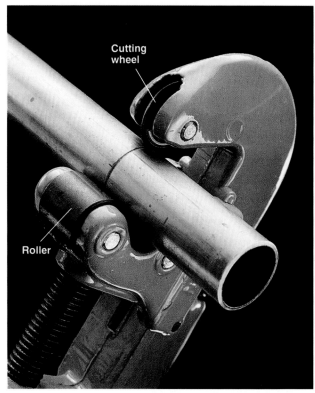

2 Turn tubing cutter one rotation so that cutting wheel scores a continuous straight line around the pipe.

3 Rotate the cutter in the opposite direction, tightening the handle slightly after every two rotations, until cut is complete.

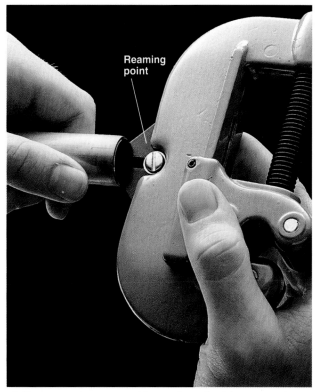

4 Remove sharp metal burrs from inside edge of the cut pipe, using the reaming point on the tubing cutter, or a round file.

How to Solder Copper Pipes & Fittings

1 Clean end of each pipe by sanding with emery cloth. Ends must be free of dirt and grease to ensure that the solder forms a good seal.

Emery cloth

2 Clean inside of each fitting by scouring with a wire brush or emery cloth.

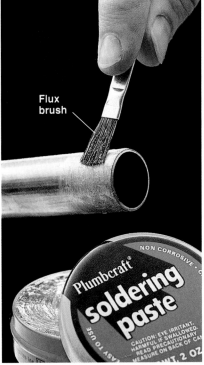

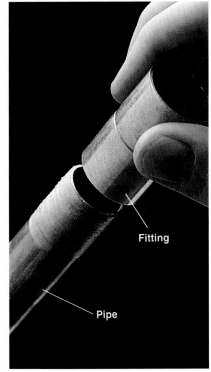

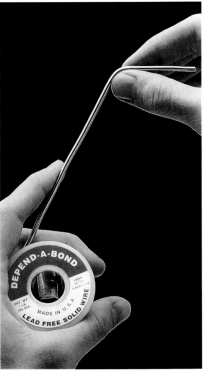

Flux brush

Fitting

Pipe

3 Apply a thin layer of soldering paste (flux) to end of each pipe, using a flux brush. Soldering paste should cover about 1" of pipe end.

4 Assemble each joint by inserting the pipe into fitting so it is tight against the bottom of the fitting sockets. Twist each fitting slightly to spread soldering paste.

5 Prepare the wire solder by unwinding 8" to 10" of wire from spool. Bend the first 2" of the wire to a 90° angle.

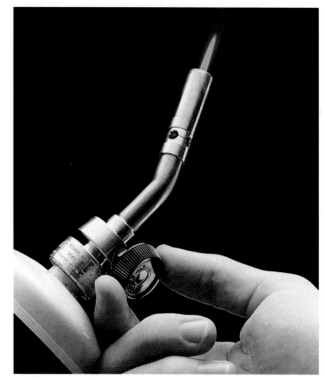

6 Light propane torch by opening valve and striking a spark lighter or a match next to the torch nozzle until the gas ignites.

7 Adjust the torch valve until the inner portion of the flame is 1" to 2" long.

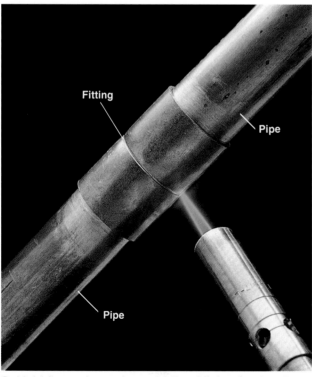

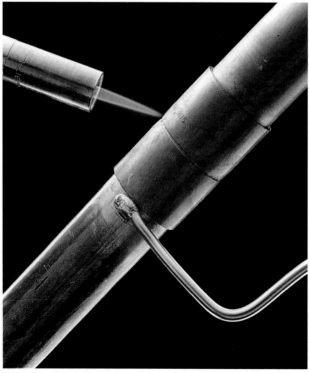

8 Hold flame tip against middle of fitting for 4 to 5 seconds, until soldering paste begins to sizzle.

9 Heat other side of copper fitting to ensure that heat is distributed evenly. Touch solder to pipe. If solder melts, pipe is ready to be soldered.

(continued next page)

How to Solder Copper Pipes & Fittings (continued)

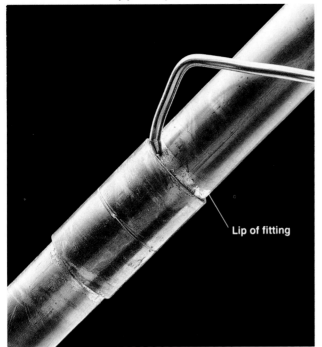

10 When pipe is hot enough to melt solder, remove torch and quickly push ½" to ¾" of solder into each joint. Capillary action fills joint with liquid solder. A correctly soldered joint should show a thin bead of solder around the lip of the fitting.

Lip of fitting

11 Wipe away excess solder with a dry rag. **Caution: pipes will be hot.** When all joints have cooled, turn on water and check for leaks. If joint leaks, drain pipes, apply additional soldering paste to rim of joint, and resolder.

How to Solder Brass Valves

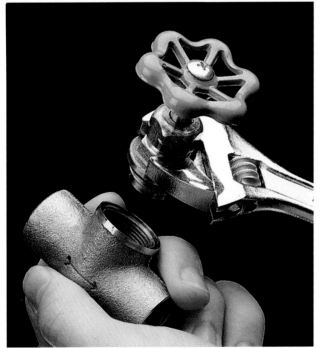

1 Remove the valve stem with an adjustable wrench. Removing the stem prevents heat damage to rubber or plastic stem parts while soldering. Prepare the copper pipes (page 22) and assemble joints.

2 Light propane torch (page 23). Heat body of valve, moving flame to distribute heat evenly. Brass is denser than copper, so it requires more heating time before joints will draw solder. Apply solder (pages 22 to 24). Let metal cool, then reassemble valve.

How to Take Apart Soldered Joints

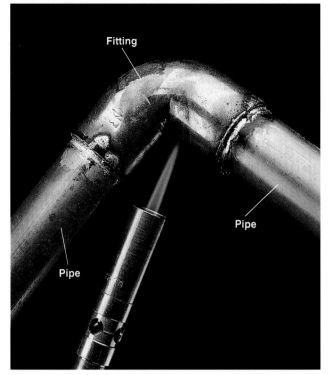

1 Turn off the water (page 6) and drain the pipes by opening the highest and lowest faucets in the house. Light propane torch (page 23). Hold flame tip to the fitting until the solder becomes shiny and begins to melt.

2 Use channel-type pliers to separate the pipes from the fitting.

3 Remove old solder by heating ends of pipe with propane torch. Use dry rag to wipe away melted solder quickly. **Caution: pipes will be hot.**

4 Use emery cloth to polish ends of pipe down to bare metal. Never reuse old fittings.

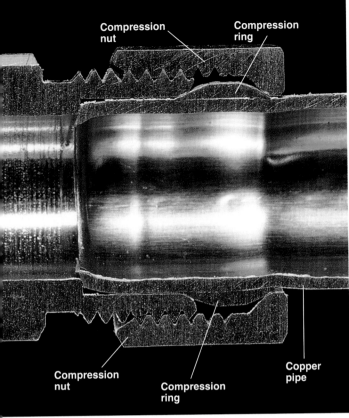

Compression
nut   Compression
             ring

Compression
nut   Compression   Copper
             ring   pipe

Compression fitting (shown in cutaway) shows how threaded compression nut forms seal by forcing the compression ring against the copper pipe. Compression ring is covered with pipe joint compound before assembling to ensure a perfect seal.

Using Compression Fittings

Compression fittings are used to make connections that may need to be taken apart. Compression fittings are easy to disconnect, and often are used to install supply tubes and fixture shutoff valves (pages 64 to 65, and sequence below). Use compression fittings in places where it is unsafe or difficult to solder, such as in a crawl space.

Compression fittings are used most often with flexible copper pipe. Flexible copper is soft enough to allow the compression ring to seat snugly, creating a watertight seal. Compression fittings also may be used to make connections with Type M rigid copper pipe. See the chart on page 18.

Everything You Need:

Tools: felt-tipped pen, tubing cutter or hacksaw, adjustable wrenches.

Materials: brass compression fittings, pipe joint compound.

How to Attach Supply Tubes to Fixture Shutoff Valves with Compression Fittings

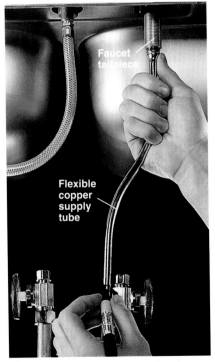

Faucet tailpiece

Flexible copper supply tube

1 Bend flexible copper supply tube, and mark to length. Include ½" for portion that will fit inside valve. Cut tube (page 21).

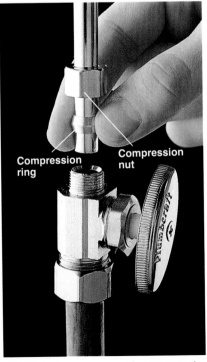

Compression ring   Compression nut

2 Slide the compression nut and then the compression ring over end of pipe. Threads of nut should face the valve.

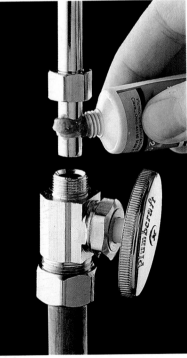

3 Apply a layer of pipe joint compound over the compression ring. Joint compound helps ensure a watertight seal.

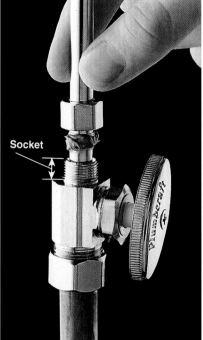

4 Insert end of pipe into fitting so it fits flush against bottom of fitting socket.

5 Slide compression ring and nut against threads of valve. Hand-tighten nut onto valve.

6 Tighten compression nut with adjustable wrenches. Do not overtighten. Turn on water and watch for leaks. If fitting leaks, tighten nut gently.

How to Join Two Copper Pipes with a Compression Union Fitting

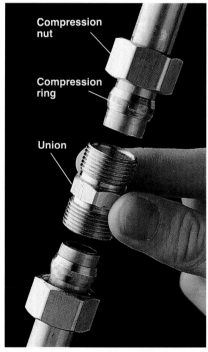

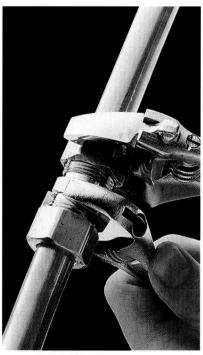

1 Slide compression nuts and rings over ends of pipes. Place threaded union between pipes.

2 Apply a layer of pipe joint compound to compression rings, then screw compression nuts onto threaded union.

3 Hold center of union fitting with an adjustable wrench, and use another wrench to tighten each compression nut one complete turn. Turn on water. If fitting leaks, tighten nuts gently.

27

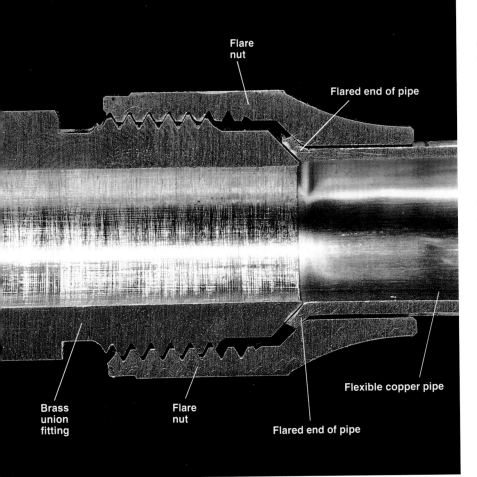

Using Flare Fittings

Flare fittings are used most often for flexible copper gas lines. Flare fittings may be used with flexible copper water supply pipes, but they cannot be used where the connections will be concealed inside walls. Always check your local codes regarding the use of flare fittings.

Flare fittings are easy to disconnect. Use a flare fitting in places where it is unsafe or difficult to solder, such as in a crawl space.

Everything You Need:

Tools: two-piece flaring tool, adjustable wrenches.

Materials: brass flare fittings.

Flare fitting (shown in cutaway) shows how flared end of flexible copper pipe forms seal against the head of a brass union fitting.

How to Join Two Copper Pipes with a Flare Union Fitting

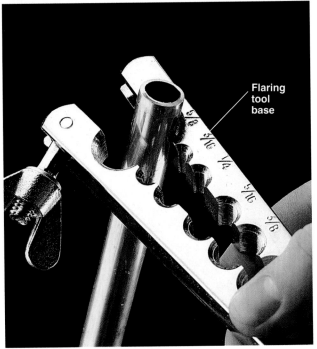

1 Slide flare nuts onto ends of pipes. Nuts must be placed on pipes before ends can be flared.

2 Select hole in flaring tool base that matches outside diameter of pipe. Open base, and place end of pipe inside hole.

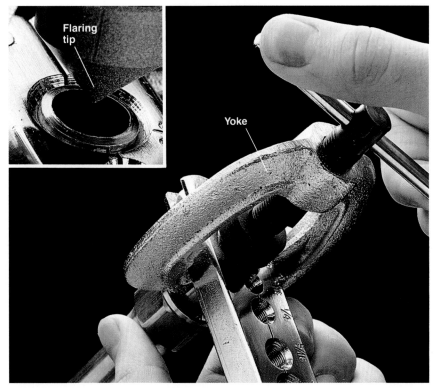

3 Clamp pipe inside flaring tool base. End of pipe must be flush with flat surface of base.

4 Slip yoke of flaring tool around base. Center flaring tip of yoke over end of pipe (inset photo above). Tighten handle of yoke to shape the end of the pipe. Flare is completed when handle cannot be turned further.

5 Remove yoke, and remove pipe from base. Repeat flaring for other pipe.

6 Place flare union between flared ends of pipe, and screw flare nuts onto union.

7 Hold center of flare union with adjustable wrench, and use another wrench to tighten flare nuts one complete turn. Turn on water. If fitting leaks, tighten nuts.

Working with Plastics

Plastic pipes and fittings are popular with do-it-yourselfers because they are lightweight, inexpensive, and easy to use. Local plumbing codes increasingly are approving the use of plastics for home plumbing.

Plastics pipes are available in rigid and flexible forms. Rigid plastics include ABS (Acrylonitrile-Butadiene-Styrene), PVC (Poly-Vinyl-Chloride), and CPVC (Chlorinated-Poly-Vinyl-Chloride). The most commonly used flexible plastic is PB (Poly-Butylene).

ABS and PVC are used in drain systems. PVC is a newer form of plastic that resists chemical damage and heat better than ABS. It is approved for above-ground use by all plumbing codes. However, some codes still require cast-iron pipe for main drains that run under concrete slabs.

CPVC and PB are used in water supply systems. Rigid CPVC pipe and fittings are less expensive than PB, but flexible PB pipe is a good choice in cramped locations, because it bends easily and requires fewer fittings.

Plastic pipes can be joined to existing iron or copper pipes using transition fittings (page 17), but different types of plastic should not be joined. For example, if your drain pipes are ABS plastic, use only ABS pipes and fittings when making repairs and replacements.

Prolonged exposure to sunlight eventually can weaken plastic plumbing pipe, so plastics should not be installed or stored in areas that receive constant direct sunlight.

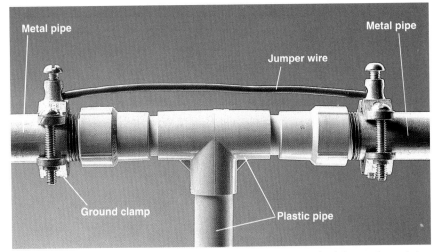

Metal pipe

Metal pipe

Jumper wire

Ground clamp

Plastic pipe

Caution: Your home electrical system could be grounded through metal water pipes. When adding plastic pipes to a metal plumbing system, make sure the electrical ground circuit is not broken. Use ground clamps and jumper wires, available at any hardware store, to bypass the plastic transition and complete the electrical ground circuit. Clamps must be firmly attached to bare metal on both sides of the plastic pipe.

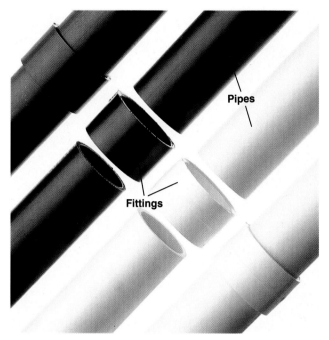

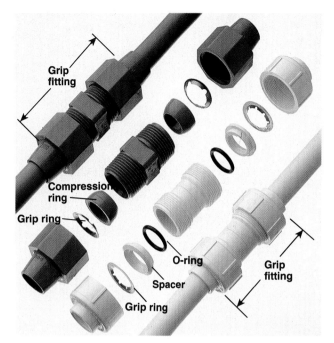

Solvent-glued fittings are used on rigid plastic pipes. Solvent dissolves a thin layer of plastic, and bonds the pipe and fitting together.

Grip fittings are used to join flexible PB pipes, and can also be used for CPVC pipes. Grip fittings come in two styles. One type (left) resembles a copper compression fitting. It has a metal grip ring and a plastic compression ring. The other type (right) has a rubber O-ring instead of a compression ring.

Plastic Pipe Grade Stamps

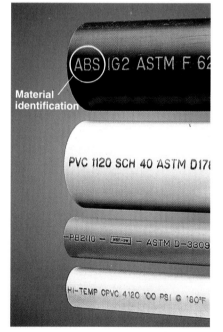

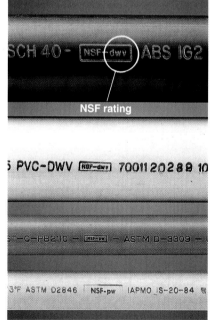

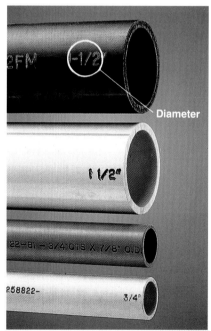

Material identification: For sink traps and drain pipes, use PVC or ABS pipe. For water supply pipes, use PB or CPVC pipe.

NSF rating: For sink traps and drains, choose PVC or ABS pipe that has a DWV (drain-waste-vent) rating from the National Sanitation Foundation (NSF). For water supply pipes, choose PB or CPVC pipe that has a PW (pressurized water) rating.

Pipe diameter: PVC and ABS pipes for drains usually have an inside diameter of 1¼" to 4". PB and CPVC pipes for water supply usually have an inside diameter of ½" or ¾".

31

Cutting & Fitting Plastic Pipe

Cut rigid ABS, PVC, or plastic pipes with a tubing cutter, or with any saw. Cuts must be straight to ensure watertight joints.

Rigid plastics are joined with plastic fittings and solvent glue. Use a solvent glue that is made for the type of plastic pipe you are installing. For example, do not use ABS solvent on PVC pipe. Some solvent glues, called "all-purpose" or "universal" solvents, may be used on all types of plastic pipe.

Solvent glue hardens in about 30 seconds, so test-fit all plastic pipes and fittings before gluing the first joint. For best results, the surfaces of plastic pipes and fittings should be dulled with emery cloth and liquid primer before they are joined.

Liquid solvent glues and primers are toxic and flammable. Provide adequate ventilation when fitting plastics, and store the products away from any source of heat.

Cut flexible PB pipes with a plastic tubing cutter, or with a knife. Make sure cut ends of pipe are straight. Join PB plastic pipes with plastic grip fittings. Grip fittings also are used to join rigid or flexible plastic pipes to copper plumbing pipes (page 17).

Everything You Need:

Tools: tape measure, felt-tipped pen, tubing cutter (or miter box or hacksaw), utility knife, channel-type pliers.

Materials: plastic pipe, fittings, emery cloth, plastic pipe primer, solvent glue, rag, petroleum jelly.

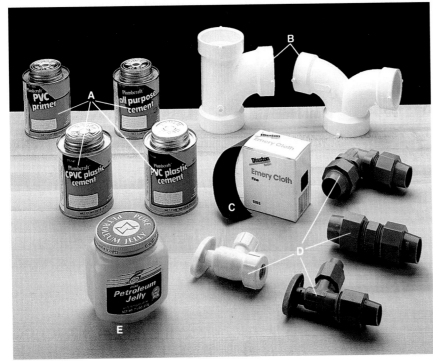

Specialty materials for plastics include: solvent glues and primer (A), solvent-glue fittings (B), emery cloth (C), plastic grip fittings (D), and petroleum jelly (E).

Measuring Plastic Pipe

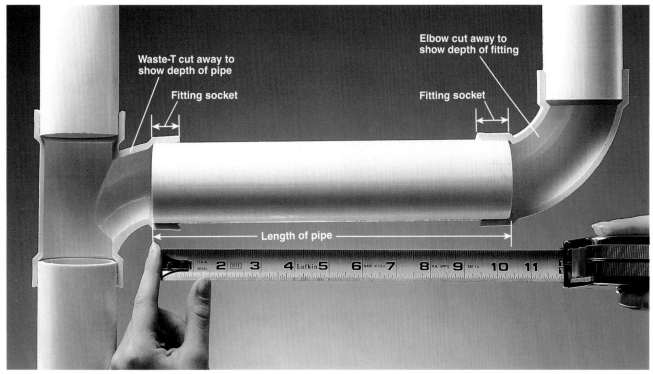

Find length of plastic pipe needed by measuring between the bottoms of the fitting sockets (fittings shown in cutaway). Mark the length on the pipe with a felt-tipped pen.

How to Cut Rigid Plastic Pipe

 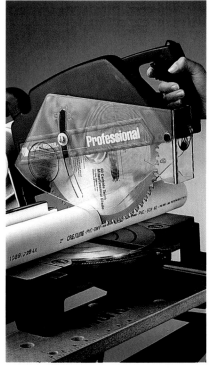 

Tubing cutter: Tighten tool around pipe so cutting wheel is on marked line (page 21). Rotate tool around pipe, tightening screw every two rotations, until pipe snaps.

Miter box: Make straight cuts on all types of plastic pipe with a power or hand miter box.

Hacksaw: Clamp plastic pipe in a portable gripping bench or a vise, and keep the hacksaw blade straight while sawing.

How to Solvent-glue Rigid Plastic Pipe

1 Remove rough burrs on cut ends of plastic pipe, using a utility knife.

2 Test-fit all pipes and fittings. Pipes should fit tightly against the bottom of the fitting sockets.

Fitting sockets

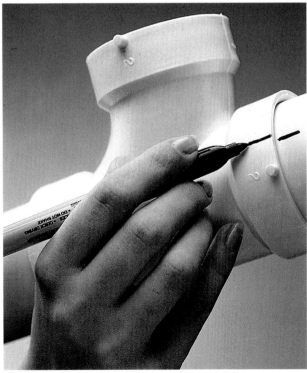

3 Make alignment marks across each joint with a felt-tipped pen.

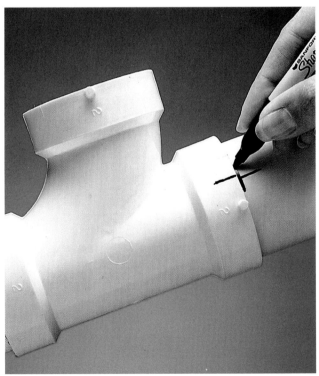

4 Mark depth of the fitting sockets on pipes. Take pipes apart.

5 Clean ends of pipes and the fitting sockets with emery cloth.

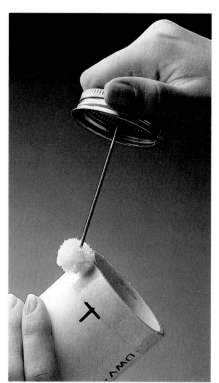

6 Apply plastic pipe primer to the ends of the pipes. Primer dulls glossy surfaces and ensures a good seal.

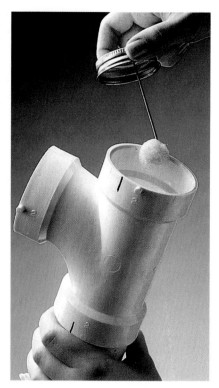

7 Apply plastic pipe primer to the insides of the fitting sockets.

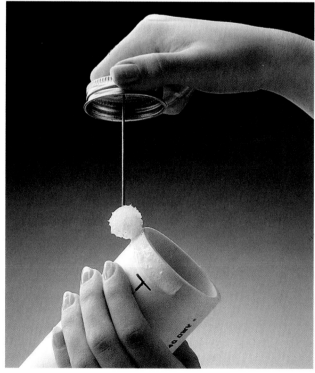

8 Solvent-glue each joint by applying a thick coat of solvent glue to end of pipe. Apply a thin coat of solvent glue to inside surface of fitting socket. Work quickly: solvent glue hardens in about 30 seconds.

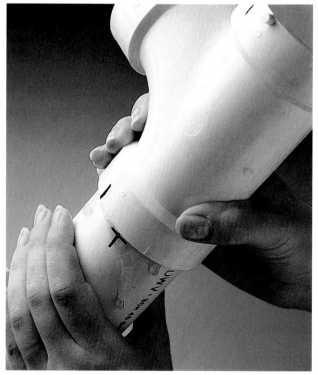

9 Quickly position pipe and fitting so that alignment marks are offset by about 2 inches. Force pipe into fitting until the end fits flush against the bottom of the socket. Twist pipe into alignment (step 10).

(continued next page)

How to Solvent-glue Rigid Plastic Pipe (continued)

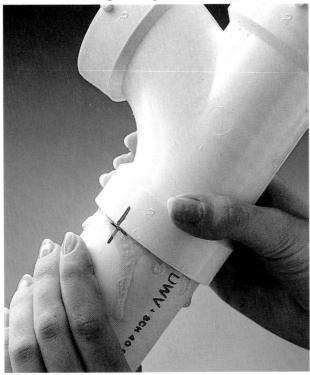

10 Spread solvent by twisting the pipe until marks are aligned. Hold pipe in place for about 20 seconds to prevent joint from slipping.

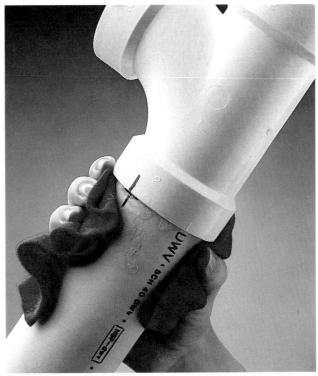

11 Wipe away excess solvent glue with a rag. Do not disturb joint for 30 minutes after gluing.

How to Cut & Fit Flexible Plastic Pipe

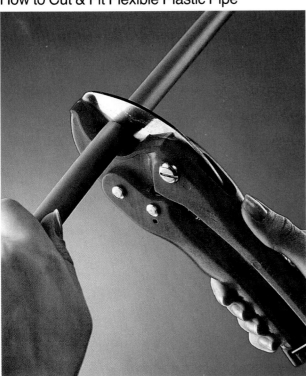

1 Cut flexible PB pipe with a plastic tubing cutter, available at home centers. (Flexible pipe also can be cut with a miter box or a sharp knife.) Remove any rough burrs with a utility knife.

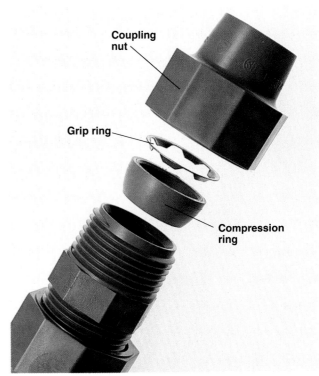

Coupling nut

Grip ring

Compression ring

2 Take each grip fitting apart and make sure that the grip ring and the compression ring or O-ring are positioned properly (page 31). Loosely reassemble the fitting.

3 Make a mark on the pipe showing the depth of the fitting socket, using a felt-tipped pen. Round off the edges of the pipe with emery cloth.

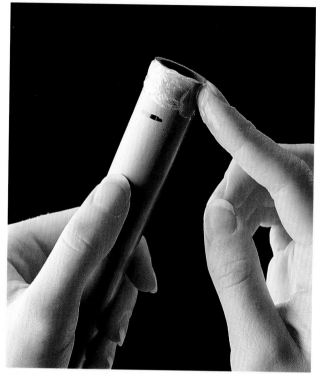

4 Lubricate the end of the pipe with petroleum jelly. Lubricated tip makes it easier to insert pipes into grip fittings.

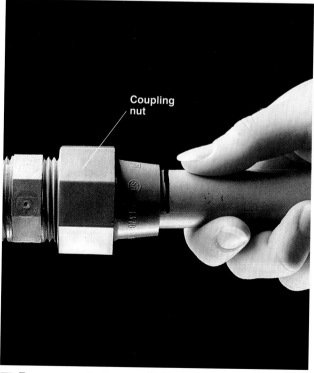

Coupling nut

5 Force end of pipe into fitting up to the mark on the pipe. Hand-tighten coupling nut.

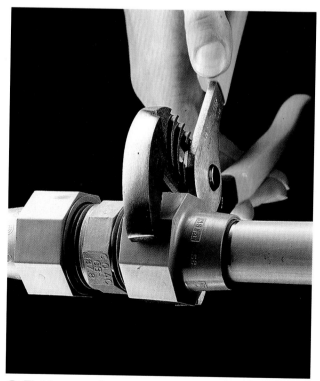

6 Tighten coupling nut about ½ turn with channel-type pliers. Turn on water and test the fitting. If the fitting leaks, tighten coupling nut slightly.

Working with Galvanized Iron

Galvanized iron pipe often is found in older homes, where it is used for water supply and small drain lines. It can be identified by the zinc coating that gives it a silver color, and by the threaded fittings used to connect pipes.

Galvanized iron pipes and fittings will corrode with age and eventually must be replaced. Low water pressure may be a sign that the insides of galvanized pipes have a buildup of rust. Blockage usually occurs in elbow fittings. Never try to clean the insides of galvanized iron pipes. Instead, remove and replace them as soon as possible.

Galvanized iron pipe and fittings are available at hardware stores and home improvement centers. Always specify the interior diameter (I.D.) when purchasing galvanized pipes and fittings. Pre-threaded pipes, called *nipples,* are available in lengths from 1" to 1 foot. If you need a longer length, have the store cut and thread the pipe to your dimensions.

Old galvanized iron can be difficult to repair. Fittings often are rusted in place, and what seems like a small job may become a large project. For example, cutting apart a section of pipe to replace a leaky fitting may reveal that adjacent pipes are also in need of replacement. If your job takes an unexpected amount of time, you can cap off any open lines and restore water to the rest of your house. Before you begin a repair, have on hand nipples and end caps that match your pipes.

Taking apart a system of galvanized iron pipes and fittings is time-consuming. Disassembly must start at the end of a pipe run, and each piece must be unscrewed before the next piece can be removed. Reaching the middle of a run to replace a section of pipe can be a long and tedious job. Instead, use a special three-piece fitting called a union. A union makes it possible to remove a section of pipe or a fitting without having to take the entire system apart.

Note: Galvanized iron is sometimes confused with "black iron." Both types have similar sizes and fittings. Black iron is used only for gas lines.

Measure old pipe. Include ½" at each end for the threaded portion of the pipe inside fitting. Bring overall measurement to the store when shopping for replacement parts.

Everything You Need:

Tools: tape measure, reciprocating saw with metal-cutting blade or a hacksaw, pipe wrenches, propane torch, wire brush.

Materials: nipples, end caps, union fitting, pipe joint compound, replacement fittings (if needed).

How to Remove & Replace a Galvanized Iron Pipe

1 Cut through galvanized iron pipe with a reciprocating saw and a metal-cutting blade, or with a hacksaw.

2 Hold fitting with one pipe wrench, and use another wrench to remove old pipe. Jaws of wrenches should face opposite directions. Always move wrench handle toward jaw opening.

3 Remove any corroded fittings using two pipe wrenches. With jaws facing in opposite directions, use one wrench to turn fitting and the other to hold the pipe. Clean pipe threads with a wire brush.

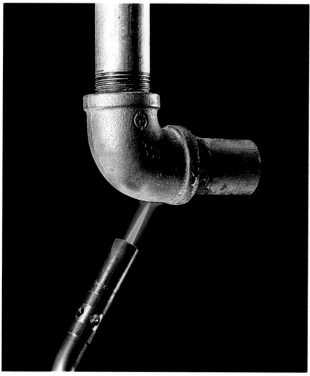

4 Heat stubborn fittings with a propane torch to make them easier to remove. Apply flame for 5 to 10 seconds. Protect wood or other flammable materials from heat, using a double layer of sheet metal (page 20).

(continued next page)

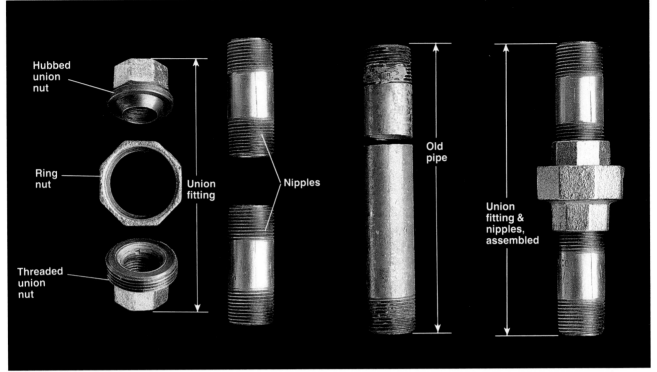

Hubbed union nut

Ring nut

Threaded union nut

Union fitting

Nipples

Old pipe

Union fitting & nipples, assembled

5 Replace a section of galvanized iron pipe with a union fitting and two threaded pipes (nipples). When assembled, the union and nipples must equal the length of the pipe that is being replaced.

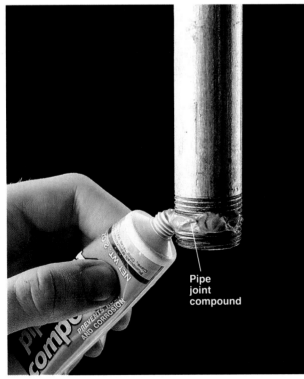

Pipe joint compound

6 Apply a bead of pipe joint compound around threaded ends of all pipes and nipples. Spread compound evenly over threads with fingertip.

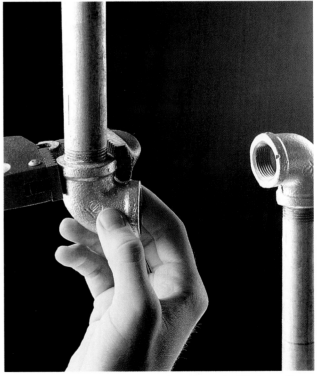

7 Screw new fittings onto pipe threads. Tighten fittings with two pipe wrenches, leaving them about 1/8 turn out of alignment to allow assembly of union.

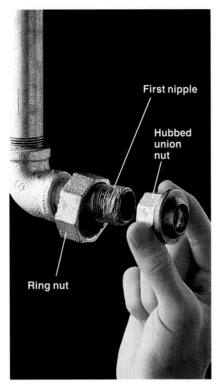

8 Screw first nipple into fitting, and tighten with pipe wrench.

9 Slide ring nut onto the installed nipple, then screw the hubbed union nut onto the nipple and tighten with a pipe wrench.

10 Screw second nipple onto other fitting. Tighten with pipe wrench.

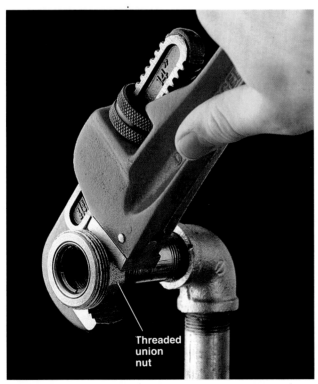

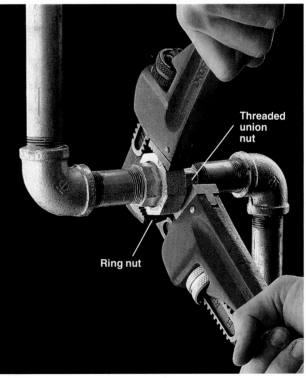

11 Screw threaded union nut onto second nipple. Tighten with a pipe wrench. Turn pipes into alignment, so that lip of hubbed union nut fits inside threaded union nut.

12 Complete the connection by screwing the ring nut onto the threaded union nut. Tighten ring nut with pipe wrenches.

Working with Cast Iron

Cast-iron pipe often is found in older homes, where it is used for large drain-waste-vent pipes, especially the main stack and sewer service lines. It can be identified by its dark color, rough surface, and large size. Cast-iron pipes in home drains usually are 3" or more in diameter.

Cast-iron pipes may rust through or hubbed fittings (below) may leak. If your house is more than 30 years old, you may find it necessary to replace a cast-iron pipe or joint.

Cast iron is heavy and difficult to cut and fit. One 5-ft. section of 4" pipe weighs 60 pounds. For this reason, leaky cast-iron pipe usually is replaced with a new plastic pipe of the same diameter. Plastic pipe can be joined to cast iron easily, using a banded coupling (below).

Cast iron is best cut with a rented tool called a *snap cutter.* Snap cutter designs vary, so follow the rental dealer's instructions for using the tool.

Everything You Need:

Tools: tape measure, chalk, adjustable wrenches, rented cast iron snap cutter (or hacksaw), ratchet wrench, screwdriver.

Materials: riser clamps or strap hangers, two wood blocks, 2½" wallboard screws, banded couplings, plastic replacement pipe.

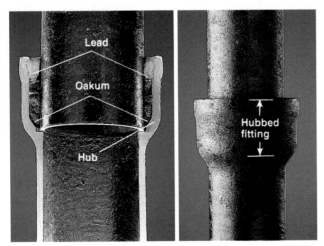

Hubbed fittings (shown cut away, left) may be used to join old cast-iron pipe. Hubbed pipe has a straight end and a flared end. The straight end of one pipe fits inside the hub of the next pipe. Joints are sealed with packing material (oakum) and lead. Repair leaky joints by cutting out the entire hubbed fitting and replacing with plastic pipe.

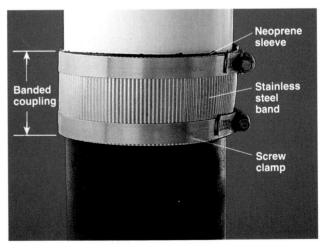

Banded couplings may be used to replace leaky cast-iron pipe with a PVC or ABS plastic pipe. The new plastic pipe is connected to the remaining cast-iron pipe with banded coupling. Banded coupling has a neoprene sleeve that seals the joint. Pipes are held together with stainless steel bands and screw clamps.

Before cutting a horizontal run of cast-iron drain pipe, make sure it is supported with strap hangers every 5 feet and at every joint connection.

Before cutting a vertical run of cast-iron pipe, make sure it is supported at every floor level with a riser clamp. Never cut apart pipe that is not supported.

How to Repair & Replace a Section of Cast-iron Pipe

1 Use chalk to mark cut lines on the cast-iron pipe. If replacing a leaky hub, mark at least 6" on each side of hub.

2 Support lower section of pipe by installing a riser clamp flush against bottom plate or floor.

3 Support upper section of pipe by installing a riser clamp 6" above pipe section to be replaced. Attach wood blocks to the studs with 2½" wallboard screws, so that the riser clamp rests on tops of blocks.

(continued next page)

How to Repair & Replace a Section of Cast-iron Pipe (continued)

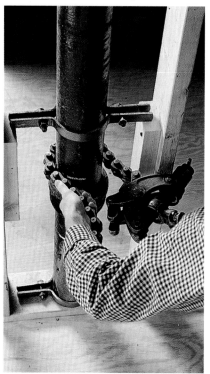

4 Wrap chain of the cast iron cutter around the pipe, so that the cutting wheels are against chalk line.

5 Tighten the chain and snap the pipe according to the tool manufacturer's directions.

6 Repeat cutting at the other chalk line. Remove cut section of pipe.

7 Cut a length of PVC or ABS plastic pipe that is about 1'' shorter than section of cast-iron pipe that has been cut away.

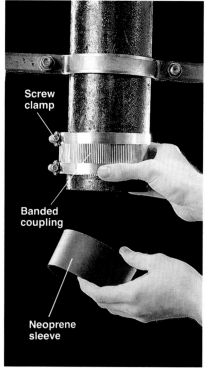

Screw clamp

Banded coupling

Neoprene sleeve

8 Slip a banded coupling and a neoprene sleeve onto each end of the cast-iron pipe.

9 Make sure the cast-iron pipe is seated snugly against the rubber separator ring molded into the interior of the sleeve.

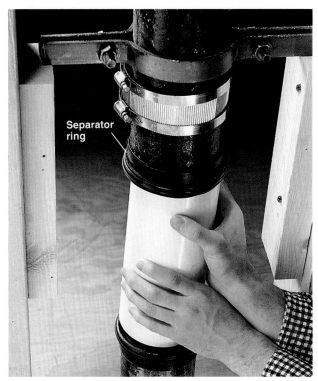

10 Fold back the end of each neoprene sleeve, until the molded separator ring on the inside of the sleeve is visible.

11 Position the new plastic pipe so it is aligned with the cast-iron pipes.

12 Roll the ends of the neoprene sleeves over the ends of the new plastic pipe.

13 Slide stainless steel bands and clamps over the neoprene sleeves.

14 Tighten the screw clamps with a ratchet wrench or screwdriver.

PRICE
PFISTER

Faucet Problems & Repairs

Most faucet problems are easy to fix. You can save money and time by making these simple repairs yourself. Replacement parts for faucet repairs usually are inexpensive and readily available at hardware stores and home centers. Techniques for repair vary, depending on the faucet design (pages 48 to 49).

If a badly worn faucet continues to leak, even after repairs are made, the faucet should be replaced. In less than an hour, you can replace an old, problem faucet with a new model that is designed to provide years of trouble-free service.

Problems	Repairs
Faucet drips from the end of the spout, or leaks around the base.	Identify the faucet design (page 49), then install replacement parts, using directions on following pages.
Old, worn-out faucet continues to leak after repairs are made.	Replace the old faucet (pages 60 to 63).
Water pressure at spout seems low, or water flow is partially blocked.	1. Clean faucet aerator (page 66). 2. Replace corroded galvanized pipes with copper (pages 20 to 29).
Water pressure from sprayer seems low, or sprayer leaks from handle.	1. Clean sprayer head (page 66). 2. Fix diverter valve (page 67).
Water leaks onto floor underneath faucet.	1. Replace cracked sprayer hose (page 67). 2. Tighten water connections, or replace supply tubes and shutoff valves (pages 64 to 65). 3. Fix leaky sink strainer (page 87).
Hose bib or valve drips from spout or leaks around handle.	Take valve apart and replace washers and O-rings (pages 68 to 69).

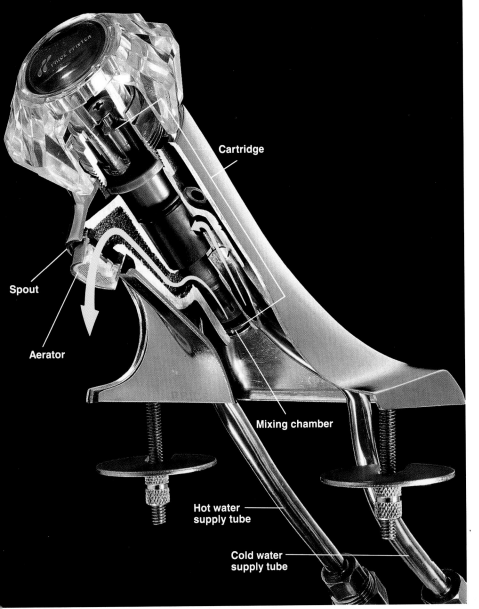

Cartridge

Spout

Aerator

Mixing chamber

Hot water
supply tube

Cold water
supply tube

Typical faucet has a single handle attached to a hollow cartridge. The cartridge controls hot and cold water flowing from the supply tubes into the mixing chamber. Water is forced out the spout and through the aerator. When repairs are needed, replace the entire cartridge.

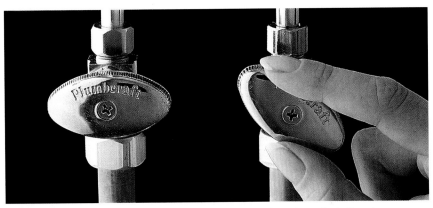

Turn off water before starting any faucet repair, using shutoff valves underneath faucet, or main service valve found near water meter (page 6). When opening shutoff valves after finishing repairs, keep faucet handle in open position to release trapped air. When water runs steadily, close faucet.

Fixing Leaky Faucets

A leaky faucet is the most common home plumbing problem. Leaks occur when washers, O-rings, or seals inside the faucet are dirty or worn. Fixing leaks is easy, but the techniques for making repairs will vary, depending on the design of the faucet. Before beginning work, you must first identify your faucet design and determine what replacement parts are needed.

There are four basic faucet designs: ball-type, cartridge, disc, or compression. Many faucets can be identified easily by outer appearance, but others must be taken apart before the design can be recognized.

The compression design is used in many double-handle faucets. Compression faucets all have washers or seals that must be replaced from time to time. These repairs are easy to make, and replacement parts are inexpensive.

Ball-type, cartridge, and disc faucets are all known as washerless faucets. Many washerless faucets are controlled with a single handle, although some cartridge models use two handles. Washerless faucets are more trouble-free than compression faucets, and are designed for quick repair.

When installing new faucet parts, make sure the replacements match the original parts. Replacement parts for popular washerless faucets are identified by brand name and model number. To ensure a correct selection, you may want to bring the worn parts to the store for comparison.

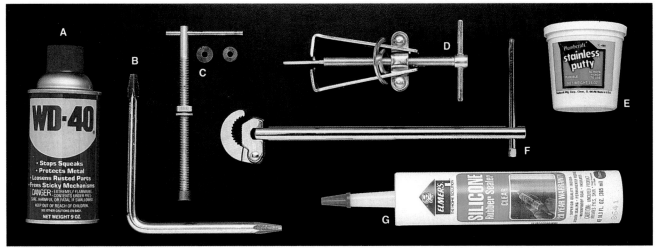

Specialty tools and materials for faucet repairs include: penetrating oil (A), seat wrench (B), seat-dressing (reamer) tool (C), handle puller (D), plumber's putty (E), basin wrench (F), silicone caulk (G).

How to Identify Faucet Designs

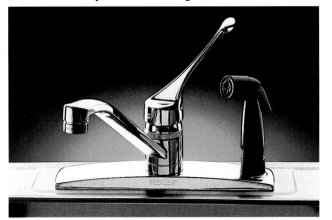

Ball-type faucet has a single handle over a dome-shaped cap. If your single-handle faucet is made by Delta or Peerless, it is probably a ball-type faucet. See pages 50 to 51 to fix a ball-type faucet.

Cartridge faucets are available in single-handle or double-handle models. Popular cartridge faucet brands include Price Pfister, Moen, Valley, and Aqualine. See pages 52 to 53 to fix a cartridge faucet.

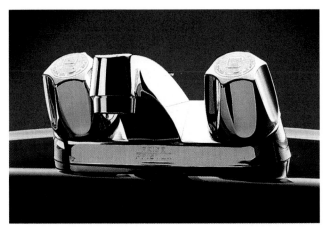

Compression faucet has two handles. When shutting the faucet off, you usually can feel a rubber washer being squeezed inside the faucet. Compression faucets are sold under many brand names. See pages 54 to 57 to fix a compression faucet.

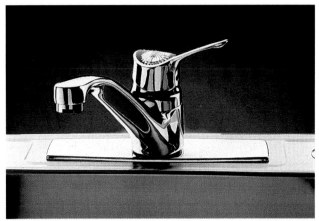

Disc faucet has a single handle and a solid, chromed-brass body. If your faucet is made by American Standard or Reliant, it may be a disc faucet. See pages 58 to 59 to fix a disc faucet.

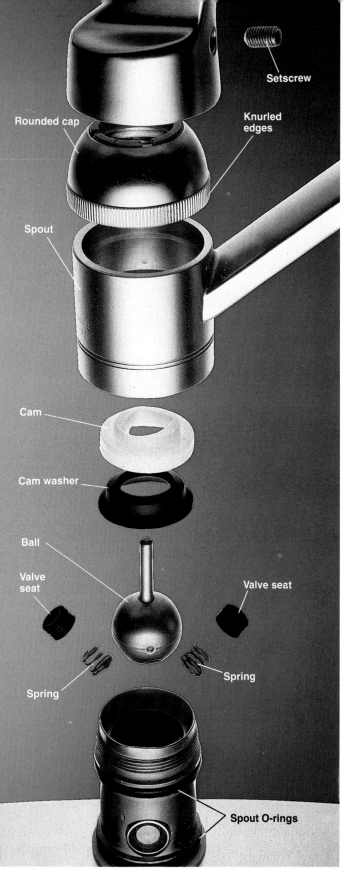

Fixing Ball-type Faucets

A ball-type faucet has a single handle, and is identified by the hollow metal or plastic ball inside the faucet body. Many ball-type faucets have a rounded cap with knurled edges located under the handle. If your faucet leaks from the spout and has this type of cap, first try tightening the cap with channel-type pliers. If tightening does not fix the leak, disassemble the faucet and install replacement parts.

Faucet manufacturers offer several types of replacement kits for ball-type faucets. Some kits contain only the springs and neoprene valve seats, while better kits also include the cam and cam washer.

Replace the rotating ball only if it is obviously worn or scratched. Replacement balls are either metal or plastic. Metal balls are slightly more expensive than plastic, but are more durable.

Remember to turn off the water before beginning work (page 48).

Everything You Need:

Tools: channel-type pliers, allen wrench, screwdriver, utility knife.

Materials: ball-type faucet repair kit, new rotating ball (if needed), masking tape, O-rings, heatproof grease.

Ball-type faucet has a hollow ball that controls the temperature and flow of water. Dripping at the faucet spout is caused by worn-out valve seats, springs, or a damaged ball. Leaks around the base of the faucet are caused by worn O-rings.

Repair kit for a ball-type faucet includes rubber valve seats, springs, cam, cam washer, and spout O-rings. Kit may also include small allen wrench tool used to remove faucet handle. Make sure kit is made for your faucet model. Replacement ball can be purchased separately, but is not needed unless old ball is obviously worn.

How to Fix a Ball-type Faucet

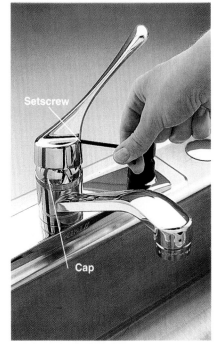

1 Loosen handle setscrew with an allen wrench. Remove handle to expose faucet cap.

2 Remove the cap with channel-type pliers. To prevent scratches to the shiny chromed finish, wrap masking tape around the jaws of the pliers.

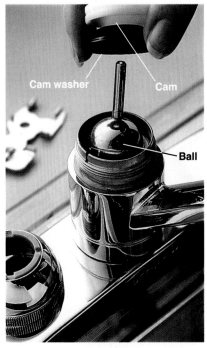

3 Lift out the faucet cam, cam washer, and the rotating ball. Check the ball for signs of wear.

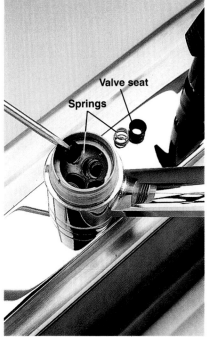

4 Reach into the faucet with a screwdriver and remove the old springs and neoprene valve seats.

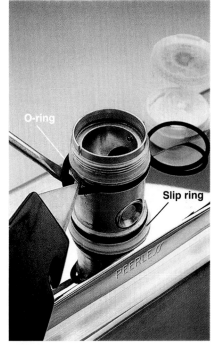

5 Remove spout by twisting it upward, then cut off old O-rings. Coat new O-rings with heatproof grease, and install. Reattach spout, pressing downward until the collar rests on plastic slip ring. Install new springs and valve seats.

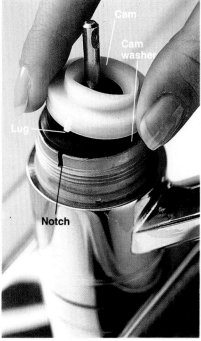

6 Insert ball, new cam washer, and cam. Small lug on cam should fit into notch on faucet body. Screw cap onto faucet and attach handle.

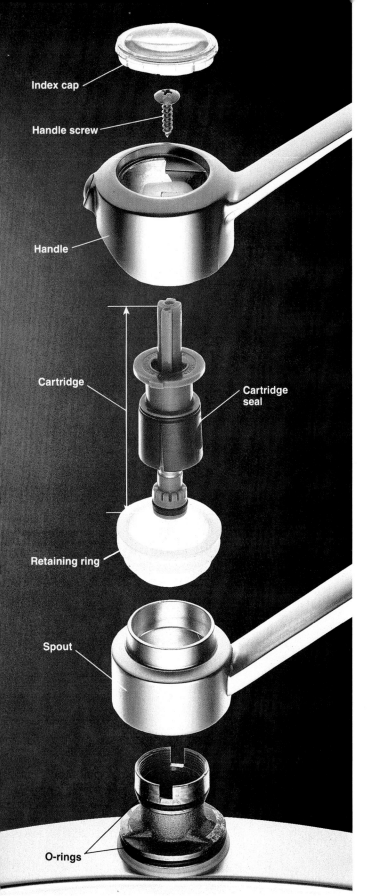

Index cap

Handle screw

Handle

Cartridge

Cartridge seal

Retaining ring

Spout

O-rings

Cartridge faucet has a hollow cartridge insert that lifts and rotates to control the flow and temperature of water. Dripping at the spout occurs when the cartridge seals become worn. Leaks around the base of the faucet are caused by worn O-rings.

Fixing Cartridge Faucets

A cartridge faucet is identified by the narrow metal or plastic cartridge inside the faucet body. Many single-handle faucets and some double-handle models use cartridge designs.

Replacing a cartridge is an easy repair that will fix most faucet leaks. Faucet cartridges come in many styles, so you may want to bring the old cartridge along for comparison when shopping for a replacement.

Make sure to insert the new cartridge so it is aligned in the same way as the old cartridge. If the hot and cold water controls are reversed, take the faucet apart and rotate the cartridge 180°.

Remember to turn off the water before beginning work (page 48).

Everything You Need:

Tools: screwdriver, channel-type pliers, utility knife.

Materials: replacement cartridge, O-rings, heatproof grease.

Replacement cartridges come in dozens of styles. Cartridges are available for popular faucet brands, including (from left): Price-Pfister, Moen, Kohler. O-ring kits may be sold separately.

How to Fix a Cartridge Faucet

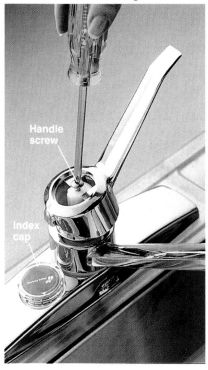

1 Pry off the index cap on top of faucet, and remove the handle screw underneath the cap.

2 Remove faucet handle by lifting it up and tilting it backwards.

3 Remove the threaded retaining ring with channel-type pliers. Remove any retaining clip holding cartridge in place.

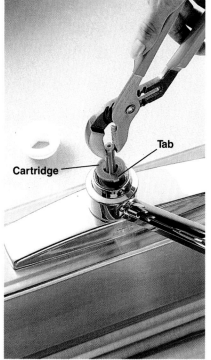

4 Grip top of the cartridge with channel-type pliers. Pull straight up to remove cartridge. Install replacement cartridge so that tab on cartridge faces forward.

5 Remove the spout by pulling up and twisting, then cut off old O-rings with a utility knife. Coat new O-rings with heatproof grease, and install.

6 Reattach the spout. Screw the retaining ring onto the faucet, and tighten with channel-type pliers. Attach the handle, handle screw, and index cap.

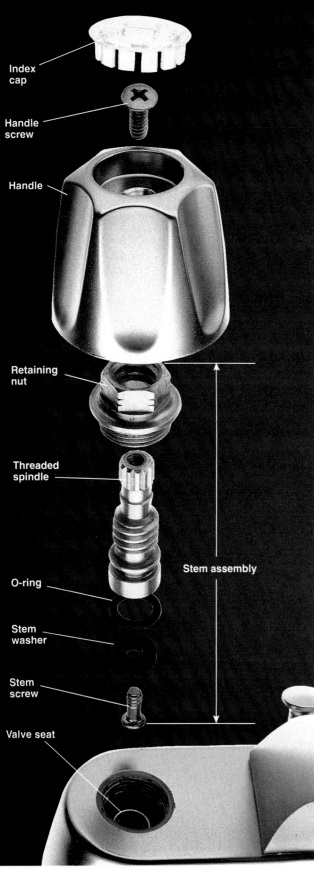

Index cap

Handle screw

Handle

Retaining nut

Threaded spindle

O-ring

Stem washer

Stem screw

Valve seat

Stem assembly

Fixing Compression Faucets

Compression faucets have separate controls for hot and cold water, and are identified by the threaded stem assemblies inside the faucet body. Compression stems come in many different styles, but all have some type of neoprene washer or seal to control water flow. Compression faucets leak when stem washers and seals become worn.

Older compression faucets often have corroded handles that are difficult to remove. A specialty tool called a handle puller makes this job easier. Handle pullers may be available at rental centers.

When replacing washers, also check the condition of the metal valve seats inside the faucet body. If the valve seats feel rough, they should be replaced or resurfaced.

Remember to turn off the water before beginning work (page 48).

Everything You Need:

Tools: screwdriver, handle puller (if needed), channel-type pliers, utility knife, seat wrench or seat-dressing tool (if needed).

Materials: universal washer kit, packing string, heatproof grease, replacement valve seats (if needed).

A compression faucet has a stem assembly that includes a retaining nut, threaded spindle, O-ring, stem washer, and stem screw. Dripping at the spout occurs when the washer becomes worn. Leaks around the handle are caused by a worn O-ring.

Universal washer kit contains parts needed to fix most types of compression faucets. Choose a kit that has an assortment of neoprene washers, O-rings, packing washers, and brass stem screws.

Tips for Fixing a Compression Faucet

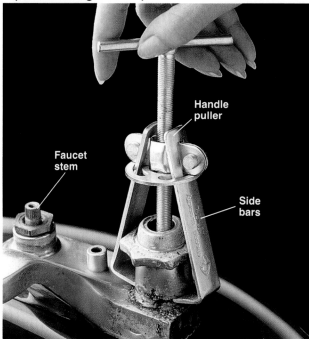

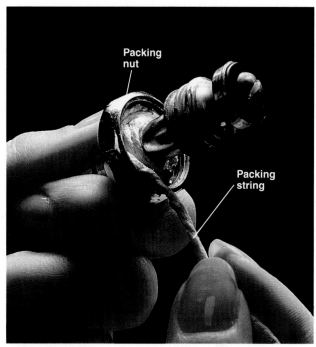

Remove stubborn handles with a handle puller. Remove the faucet index cap and handle screw, and clamp the side bars of the puller under the handle. Thread the puller into the faucet stem, and tighten until the handle comes free.

Packing string is used instead of an O-ring on some faucets. To fix leaks around the faucet handle, wrap new packing string around the stem, just underneath the packing nut or retaining nut.

Three Common Types of Compression Stems

Standard stem has a brass stem screw that holds either a flat or beveled neoprene washer to the end of the spindle. If stem screw is worn, it should be replaced.

Tophat stem has a snap-on neoprene diaphragm instead of a standard washer. Fix leaks by replacing the diaphragm.

Reverse-pressure stem has a beveled washer at the end of the spindle. To replace washer, unscrew spindle from rest of the stem assembly. Some stems have a small nut that holds washer.

How to Fix a Compression Faucet

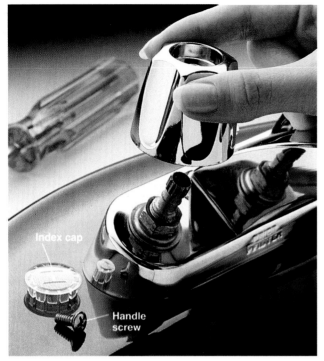

1 Remove index cap from top of faucet handle, and remove handle screw. Remove handle by pulling straight up. If necessary, use a handle puller to remove handle (page 55).

2 Unscrew the stem assembly from body of faucet, using channel-type pliers. Inspect valve seat for wear, and replace or resurface as needed (page opposite). If faucet body or stems are badly worn, it usually is best to replace the faucet (pages 60 to 63).

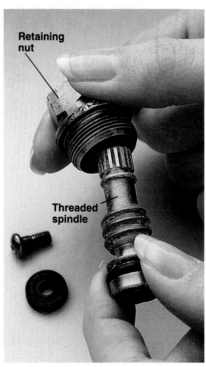

3 Remove the brass stem screw from the stem assembly. Remove worn stem washer.

4 Unscrew the threaded spindle from the retaining nut.

5 Cut off O-ring and replace with an exact duplicate. Install new washer and stem screw. Coat all parts with heatproof grease, then reassemble the faucet.

How to Replace Worn Valve Seats

1 Check valve seat for damage by running a fingertip around the rim of the seat. If the valve seat feels rough, replace the seat, or resurface it with a seat-dressing (reamer) tool (below).

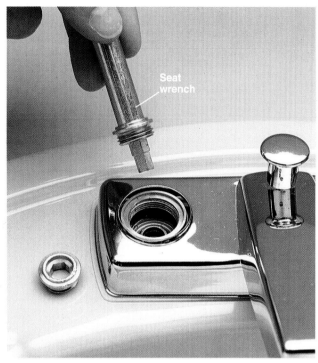

2 Remove valve seat, using a seat wrench. Select end of wrench that fits seat, and insert into faucet. Turn counterclockwise to remove seat, then install an exact duplicate. If seat cannot be removed, resurface with a seat-dressing tool (below).

How to Resurface Valve Seats

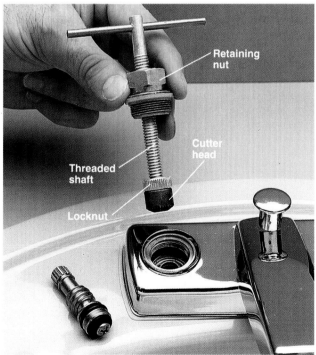

1 Select cutter head to fit the inside diameter of retaining nut. Slide retaining nut over threaded shaft of seat-dressing tool, then attach the locknut and cutter head to the shaft.

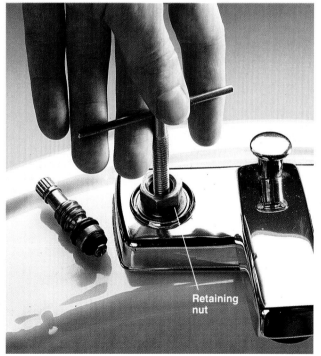

2 Screw retaining nut loosely into faucet body. Press the tool down lightly and turn tool handle clockwise two or three rotations. Reassemble faucet.

Fixing Disc Faucets

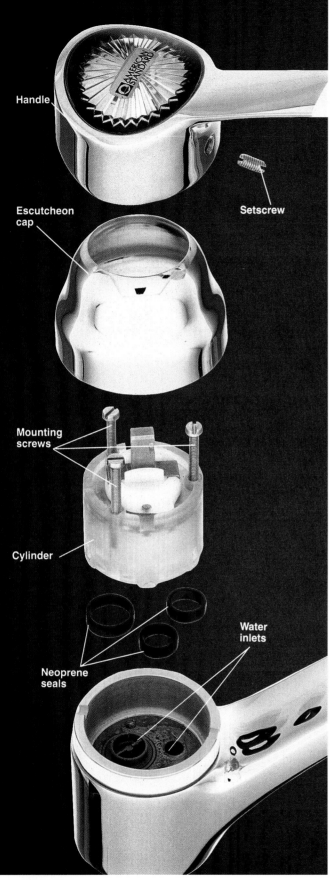

A disc faucet has a single handle and is identified by the wide cylinder inside the faucet body. The cylinder contains a pair of closely fitting ceramic discs that control the flow of water.

A ceramic disc faucet is a top-quality fixture that is easy to repair. Leaks usually can be fixed by lifting out the cylinder and cleaning the neoprene seals and the cylinder openings. Install a new cylinder only if the faucet continues to leak after cleaning.

After making repairs to a disc faucet, make sure handle is in the ON position, then open the shutoff valves slowly. Otherwise, ceramic discs can be cracked by the sudden release of air from the faucet. When water runs steadily, close the faucet.

Remember to turn off the water before beginning work (page 48).

Everything You Need:

Tools: screwdriver.

Materials: Scotch Brite® pad, replacement cylinder (if needed).

Disc faucet has a sealed cylinder containing two closely fitting ceramic discs. Faucet handle controls water by sliding the discs into alignment. Dripping at the spout occurs when the neoprene seals or cylinder openings are dirty.

Replacement cylinder for disc faucet is necessary only if faucet continues to leak after cleaning. Continuous leaking is caused by cracked or scratched ceramic discs. Replacement cylinders come with neoprene seals and mounting screws.

How to Fix a Ceramic Disc Faucet

1 Rotate faucet spout to the side, and raise the handle. Remove the setscrew and lift off the handle.

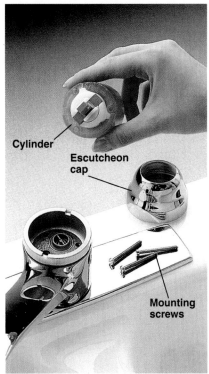

2 Remove the escutcheon cap. Remove cartridge mounting screws, and lift out the cylinder.

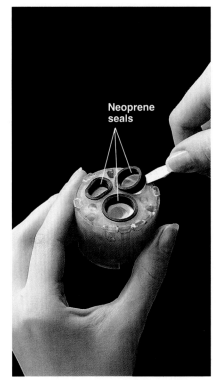

3 Remove the neoprene seals from the cylinder openings.

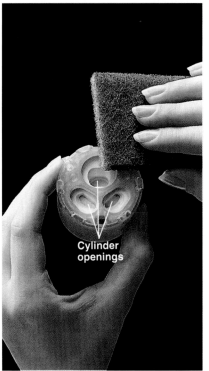

4 Clean the cylinder openings and the neoprene seals with a Scotch Brite® pad. Rinse cylinder with clear water.

5 Return seals to the cylinder openings, and reassemble faucet. Move handle to ON position, then slowly open shutoff valves. When water runs steadily, close faucet.

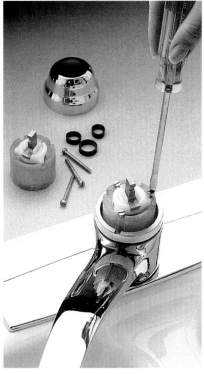

Install a new cylinder only if the faucet continues to leak after cleaning.

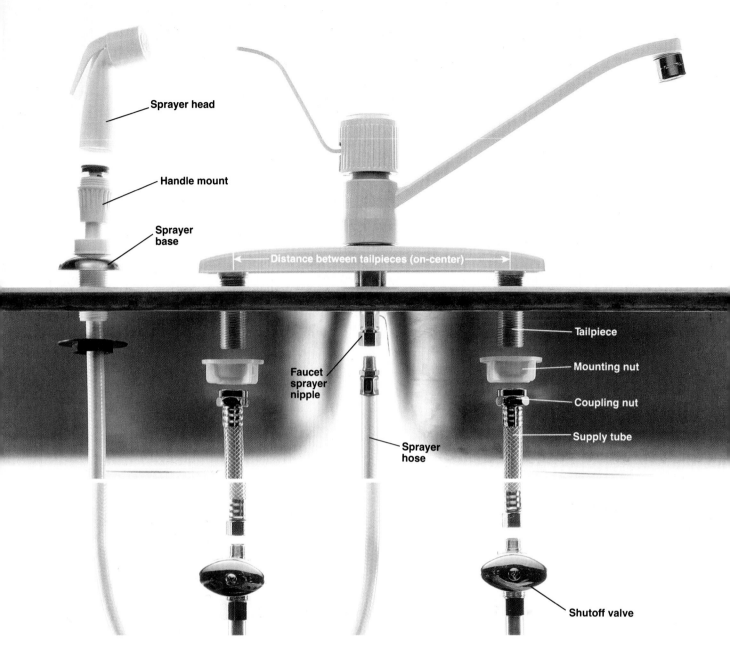

Sprayer head

Handle mount

Sprayer base

Distance between tailpieces (on-center)

Faucet sprayer nipple

Sprayer hose

Tailpiece

Mounting nut

Coupling nut

Supply tube

Shutoff valve

Replacing a Sink Faucet

Installing a new faucet is an easy project that takes about one hour. Before buying a new faucet, first find the diameter of the sink openings, and measure the distance between the tailpieces (measured on-center). Make sure the tailpieces of the new faucet match the sink openings.

When shopping for a new faucet, choose a model made by a reputable manufacturer. Replacement parts for a well-known brand will be easy to find if the faucet ever needs repairs. Better faucets have solid brass bodies. They are easy to install and provide years of trouble-free service. Some washerless models have lifetime warranties.

Always install new supply tubes when replacing a faucet. Old supply tubes should not be reused. If

water pipes underneath the sink do not have shutoff valves, you may choose to install the valves while replacing the faucet (pages 64 to 65).

Remember to turn off the water before beginning work (page 48).

Everything You Need:

Tools: basin wrench or channel-type pliers, putty knife, caulk gun, adjustable wrenches.

Materials: penetrating oil, silicone caulk or plumber's putty, two flexible supply tubes.

How to Remove an Old Sink Faucet

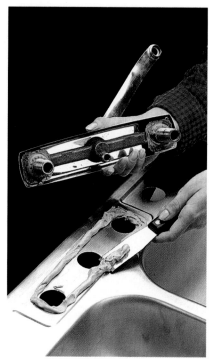

1 Spray penetrating oil on tailpiece mounting nuts and supply tube coupling nuts. Remove the coupling nuts with a basin wrench or channel-type pliers.

2 Remove the tailpiece mounting nuts with a basin wrench or channel-type pliers. Basin wrench has a long handle that makes it easy to work in tight areas.

3 Remove faucet. Use a putty knife to clean away old putty from surface of sink.

Faucet Hookup Variations

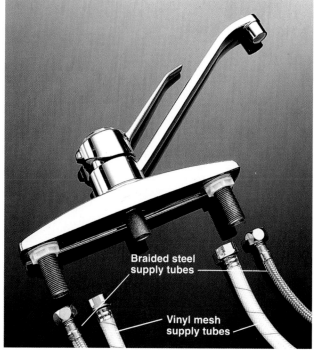

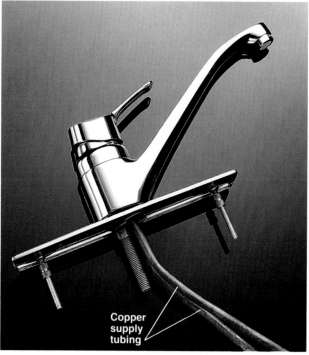

New faucet without supply tubes: Buy two supply tubes. Supply tubes are available in braided steel or vinyl mesh (shown above), PB plastic, or chromed copper (page 64).

New faucet with preattached copper supply tubing: Make water connections by attaching the supply tubing directly to the shutoff valves with compression fittings (page 63).

How to Install a New Sink Faucet

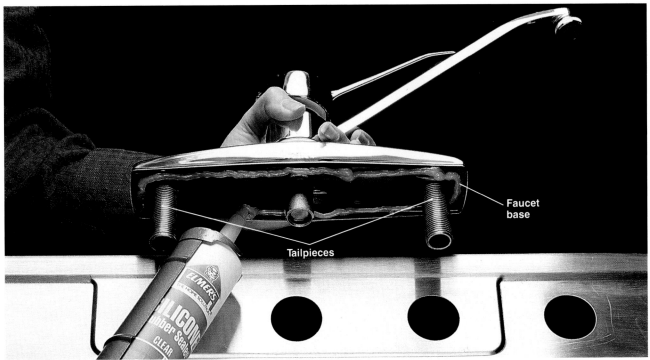

1 Apply a ¼'' bead of silicone caulk or plumber's putty around the base of the faucet. Insert the faucet tailpieces into the sink openings. Position the faucet so base is parallel to back of sink, and press the faucet down to make sure caulk forms a good seal.

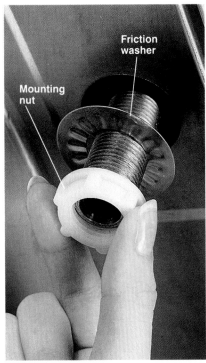

2 Screw the metal friction washers and the mounting nuts onto the tailpieces, then tighten with a basin wrench or channel-type pliers. Wipe away excess caulk around base of faucet.

3 Connect flexible supply tubes to faucet tailpieces. Tighten coupling nuts with a basin wrench or channel-type pliers.

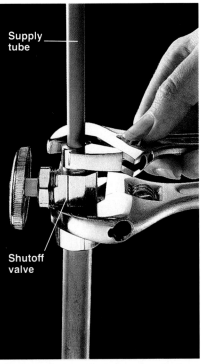

4 Attach supply tubes to shutoff valves, using compression fittings (pages 26 to 27). Hand-tighten nuts, then use an adjustable wrench to tighten nuts ¼ turn. If necessary, hold valve with another wrench while tightening.

How to Connect a Faucet with Preattached Supply Tubing

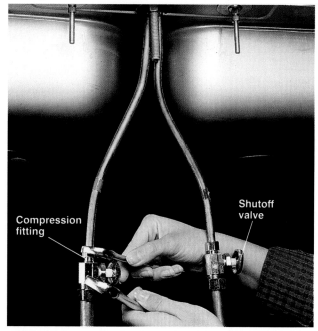

1 Attach faucet to sink by placing rubber gasket, retainer ring, and locknut onto threaded tailpiece. Tighten locknut with a basin wrench or channel-type pliers. Some center-mounted faucets have a decorative coverplate. Secure coverplate from underneath with washers and locknuts screwed onto coverplate bolts.

2 Connect preattached supply tubing to shutoff valves with compression fittings (pages 26 to 27). Red-coded tube should be attached to the hot water pipe, blue-coded tube to the cold water pipe.

How to Attach a Sink Sprayer

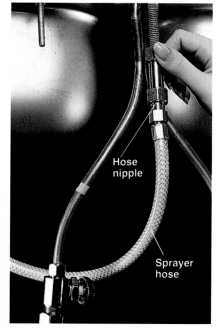

1 Apply a ¼" bead of plumber's putty or silicone caulk to bottom edge of sprayer base. Insert tailpiece of sprayer base into sink opening.

2 Place friction washer over tailpiece. Screw the mounting nut onto tailpiece and tighten with a basin wrench or channel-type pliers. Wipe away excess putty around base of sprayer.

3 Screw sprayer hose onto the hose nipple on the bottom of the faucet. Tighten ¼ turn, using a basin wrench or channel-type pliers.

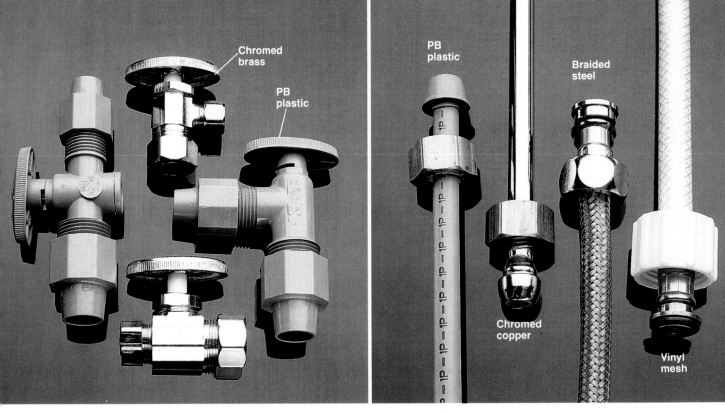

Shutoff valves allow you to shut off the water to an individual fixture so it can be repaired. They can be made from durable chromed brass or lightweight plastic. Shutoff valves come in ½" and ¾" diameters to match common water pipe sizes.

Supply tubes are used to connect water pipes to faucets, toilets, and other fixtures. They come in 12", 20", and 30" lengths. PB plastic and chromed copper tubes are inexpensive. Braided steel and vinyl mesh supply tubes are easy to install.

Installing Shutoff Valves & Supply Tubes

Worn-out shutoff valves or supply tubes can cause water to leak underneath a sink or other fixture. First, try tightening the fittings with an adjustable wrench. If this does not fix the leak, replace the shutoff valves and supply tubes.

Shutoff valves are available in several fitting types. For copper pipes, valves with compression-type fittings (pages 26 to 27) are easiest to install. For plastic pipes (pages 30 to 37), use grip-type valves. For galvanized iron pipes (pages 38 to 41), use valves with female threads.

Older plumbing systems often were installed without fixture shutoff valves. When repairing or replacing plumbing fixtures, you may want to install shutoff valves if they are not already present.

Everything You Need:

Tools: hacksaw, tubing cutter, adjustable wrench, tubing bender, felt-tipped pen.

Materials: shutoff valves, supply tubes, pipe joint compound.

How to Install Shutoff Valves & Supply Tubes

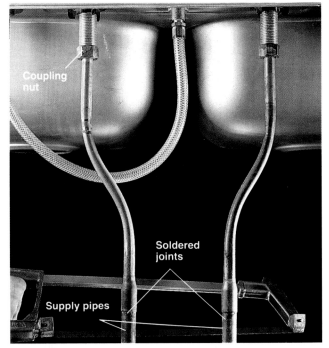

1 Turn off water at the main shutoff valve (page 6). Remove old supply pipes. If pipes are soldered copper, cut them off just below the soldered joint, using a hacksaw or tubing cutter. Make sure the cuts are straight. Unscrew the coupling nuts, and discard the old pipes.

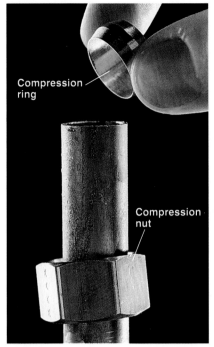

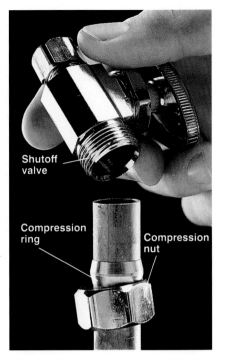

2 Slide a compression nut and compression ring over copper water pipe. Threads of nut should face end of pipe.

3 Slide shutoff valve onto pipe. Apply a layer of pipe joint compound to compression ring. Screw the compression nut onto the shutoff valve and tighten with an adjustable wrench.

4 Bend chromed copper supply tube to reach from the tailpiece of the fixture to the shutoff valve, using a tubing bender (page 19). Bend the tube slowly to avoid crimping the metal.

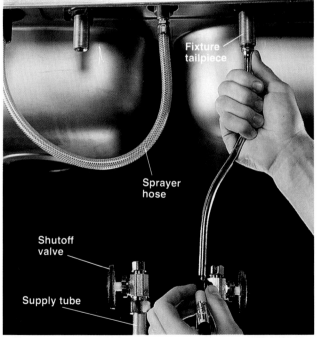

5 Position the supply tube between fixture tailpiece and shutoff valve, and mark tube to length. Cut supply tube with a tubing cutter (page 21).

6 Attach bell-shaped end of supply tube to fixture tailpiece with coupling nut, then attach other end to shutoff valve with compression ring and nut (pages 26 to 27). Tighten all fittings with adjustable wrench.

Fixing Sprayers & Aerators

If water pressure from a sink sprayer seems low, or if water leaks from the handle, it is usually because lime buildup and sediment have blocked small openings inside the sprayer head. To fix the problem, first take the sprayer head apart and clean the parts. If cleaning the sprayer head does not help, the problem may be caused by a faulty diverter valve. The diverter valve inside the faucet body shifts water flow from the faucet spout to the sprayer when the sprayer handle is pressed. Cleaning or replacing the diverter valve may fix water pressure problems.

Whenever making repairs to a sink sprayer, check the sprayer hose for kinks or cracks. A damaged hose should be replaced.

If water pressure from a faucet spout seems low, or if the flow is partially blocked, take the spout aerator apart and clean the parts. The aerator is a screw-on attachment with a small wire screen that mixes tiny air bubbles into the water flow. Make sure the wire screen is not clogged with sediment and lime buildup. If water pressure is low throughout the house, it may be because galvanized iron water pipes are corroded. Corroded pipes should be replaced with copper (pages 20 to 29).

Everything You Need:

Tools: screwdriver, channel-type pliers, needle-nose pliers, small brush.

Materials: vinegar, universal washer kit, heat-proof grease, replacement sprayer hose.

Clean faucet aerators and sink sprayers to fix most low water pressure problems. Take aerator or sprayer head apart, then use a small brush dipped in vinegar to remove sediment.

How to Fix a Diverter Valve

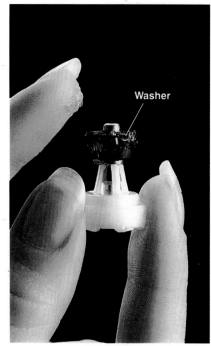

1 Shut off the water (page 48). Remove the faucet handle and the spout (see directions for your faucet type, pages 50 to 59).

2 Pull diverter valve from faucet body with needlenose pliers. Use a small brush dipped in vinegar to clean lime buildup and debris from valve.

3 Replace any worn O-rings or washers, if possible. Coat the new parts with heatproof grease, then reinstall the diverter valve and reassemble the faucet.

How to Replace a Sprayer Hose

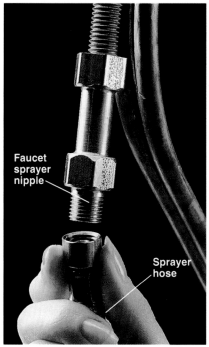

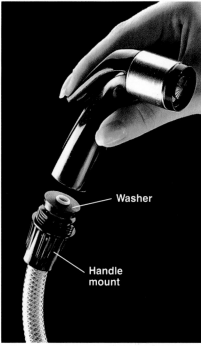

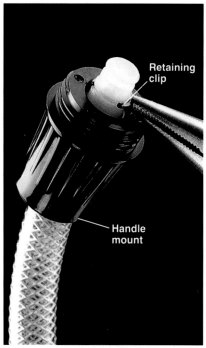

1 Unscrew sprayer hose from faucet sprayer nipple, using channel-type pliers. Pull sprayer hose through sink opening.

2 Unscrew the sprayer head from the handle mount. Remove washer.

3 Remove retainer clip with needlenose pliers, and discard old hose. Attach handle mount, retainer clip, washer, and sprayer head to new hose. Attach sprayer hose to faucet sprayer nipple on faucet.

Shutoff valve

Globe valve

Gate valve

Saddle valve

Hose bib

Repairing Valves & Hose Bibs

Valves make it possible to shut off water at any point in the supply system. If a pipe breaks or a plumbing fixture begins to leak, you can shut off water to the damaged area so that it can be repaired. A hose bib is a faucet with a threaded spout, often used to connect rubber utility or appliance hoses.

Valves and hose bibs leak when washers or seals wear out. Replacement parts can be found in the same universal washer kits used to repair compression faucets (page 54). Coat replacement washers with heatproof grease to keep them soft and prevent cracking.

Remember to turn off the water before beginning work (page 6).

Everything You Need:

Tools: screwdriver, adjustable wrench.

Materials: universal washer kit, heatproof grease.

How to Fix a Leaky Hose Bib

Packing nut

1 Remove the handle screw, and lift off the handle. Unscrew the packing nut with an adjustable wrench.

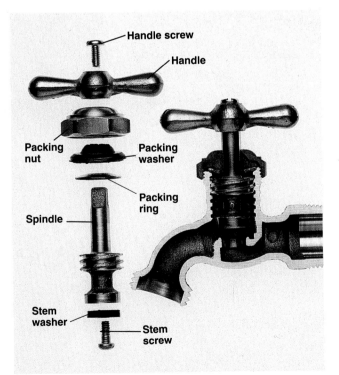

Handle screw

Handle

Packing nut

Packing washer

Packing ring

Spindle

Stem washer

Stem screw

2 Unscrew the spindle from the valve body. Remove the stem screw and replace the stem washer. Replace the packing washer, and reassemble the valve.

Common Types of Valves

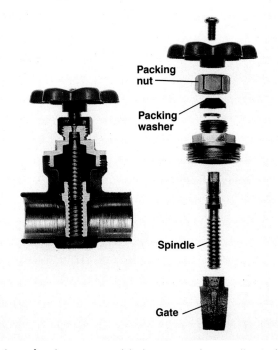

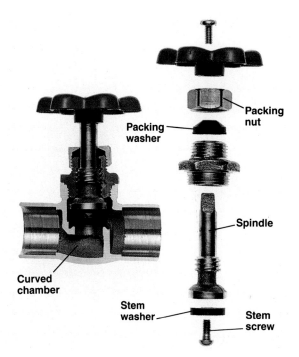

Gate valve has a movable brass wedge, or "gate," that screws up and down to control water flow. Gate valves may develop leaks around the handle. Repair leaks by replacing the packing washer or packing string found underneath the packing nut.

Globe valve has a curved chamber. Repair leaks around the handle by replacing the packing washer. If valve does not fully stop water flow when closed, replace the stem washer.

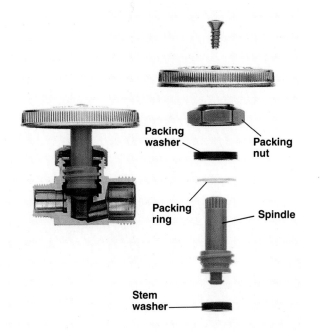

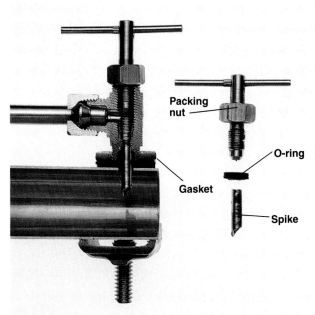

Shutoff valve controls water supply to a single fixture (pages 64 to 65). Shutoff valve has a plastic spindle with a packing washer and a snap-on stem washer. Repair leaks around the handle by replacing the packing washer. If valve does not fully stop water flow when closed, replace the stem washer.

Saddle valve is a small fitting often used to connect a refrigerator icemaker or sink-mounted water filter to a copper water pipe. Saddle valve contains a hollow metal spike that punctures water pipe when valve is first closed. Fitting is sealed with a rubber gasket. Repair leaks around the handle by replacing the O-ring under the packing nut.

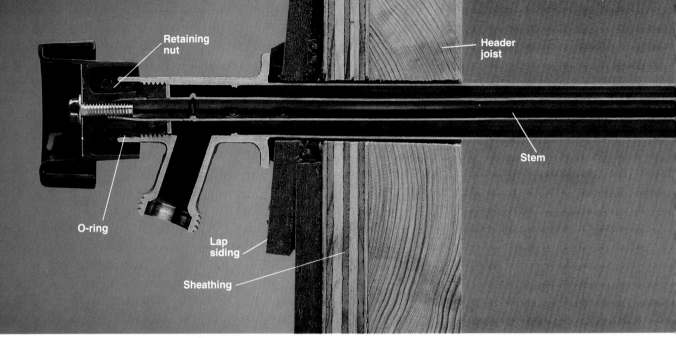

Frost-proof sillcock is mounted against the header joist (sill), and has a long stem that reaches 6" to 30" inside the house to protect the valve from cold. A sillcock should angle downward slightly to provide drainage. The stem washer and O-ring (or packing string) can be replaced if the sillcock begins to leak. In a copper plumbing system,

Installing & Repairing Sillcocks

A sillcock is a compression faucet attached to the outside of the house. Repair a leaky sillcock by replacing the stem washer and the O-ring.

Sillcocks can be damaged by frost. To repair a pipe that has ruptured due to frost, see pages 122 to 123. To prevent pipes from rupturing, close the indoor shutoff valves at the start of the cold weather season, disconnect all garden hoses, and open the sillcock to let trapped water drain out.

A special frost-proof sillcock has a long stem that reaches at least 6" inside the house to protect it from cold. Install a sillcock so the pipe angles downward from the shutoff valve. This allows water to drain away each time the faucet is turned off.

Remember to turn off the water before beginning work (page 6).

Everything You Need:

Tools: screwdriver, channel-type pliers, pencil, right-angle drill or standard drill, 1" spade bit, caulk gun, hacksaw or tubing cutter, propane torch.

Materials: universal washer kit, sillcock, silicone caulk, 2" corrosion-resistant screws, copper pipe, T-fitting, Teflon™ tape, threaded adapter, shutoff valve, emery cloth, soldering paste (flux), solder.

How to Repair a Sillcock

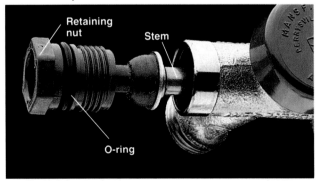

1 Remove sillcock handle, and loosen retaining nut with channel-type pliers. Remove stem. Replace O-ring found on retaining nut or stem.

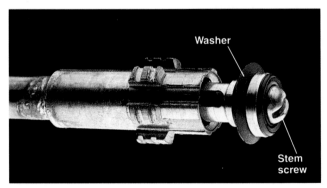

2 Remove the brass stem screw at the end of the stem, and replace the washer. Reassemble the sillcock.

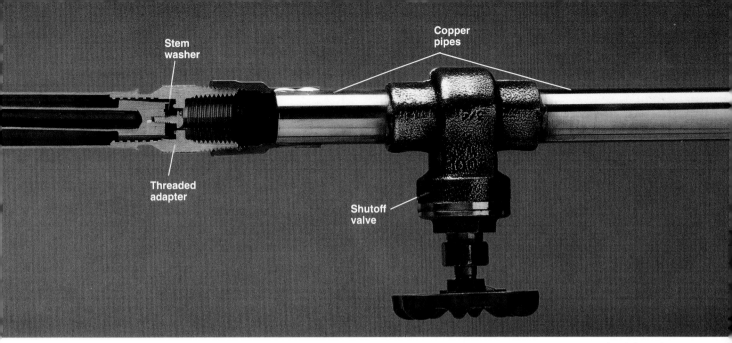

the sillcock is connected to a nearby cold water supply pipe with a threaded adapter, two lengths of soldered copper pipe, and a shutoff valve. A T-fitting (not shown) is used to tap into an existing cold water pipe.

How to Install a Frost-proof Sillcock

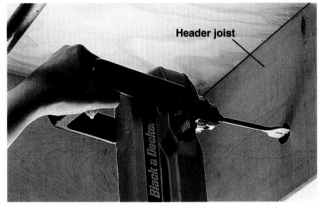

1 Locate position of hole for sillcock. From nearest cold water pipe, mark a point on header joist that is slightly lower than water pipe. Drill a hole through header, sheathing, and siding, using a 1" spade bit.

2 Apply a thick bead of silicone caulk to bottom of sillcock flange, then insert sillcock into hole, and attach to siding with 2" corrosion-resistant screws. Turn handle to ON position. Wipe away excess caulk.

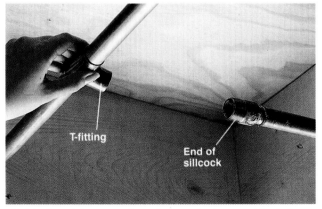

3 Mark cold water pipe, then cut pipe and install a T-fitting (pages 22 to 25). Wrap Teflon™ tape around threads of sillcock.

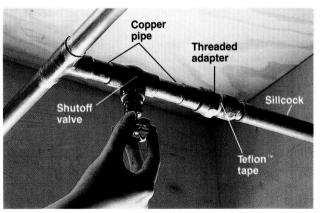

4 Join T-fitting to sillcock with a threaded adapter (page 17), a shutoff valve, and two lengths of copper pipe. Prepare pipes and solder the joints. Turn on water, and close sillcock when water runs steadily.

(1) Handle

(8) Float ball

Lift chain
(or lift wires)

**(2) Flapper
(or tank ball)**

Tank

**(3) Flush
valve**

Rim openings

**(4) Toilet
bowl**

(5) Trap

Base

Wax
ring

**(6) Main
drain**

orks: When the **handle (1)** is pushed, ...ses a rubber seal, called a **flapper or** ...ter in the tank rushes down through ...pening **(3)** in the bottom of the tank, ...wl **(4)**. Waste water in the bowl is ...the **trap (5)** into the **main drain (6)**.

When the toilet tank is empty, the flapper seals the tank, and a water supply valve, called a **ballcock (7)**, refills the toilet tank. The ballcock is controlled by a **float ball (8)** that rides on the surface of the water. When the tank is full, the float ball automatically shuts off the ballcock.

Common Toilet Problems

A clogged toilet is one of the most common plumbing problems. If a toilet overflows or flushes sluggishly, clear the clog with a plunger or closet auger (page 90). If the problem persists, the clog may be in the main waste and vent stack (page 97).

Most other toilet problems are fixed easily with minor adjustments that require no disassembly or replacement parts. You can make these adjustments in a few minutes, using simple tools (page 74).

If minor adjustments do not fix the problem, further repairs will be needed. The parts of a standard toilet are not difficult to take apart, and most repair projects can be completed in less than an hour.

A recurring puddle of water on the floor around a toilet may be caused by a crack in the toilet base or in the tank. A damaged toilet should be replaced. Installing a new toilet is an easy project that can be finished in three or four hours.

A standard two-piece toilet has an upper tank that is bolted to a base. This type of toilet uses a simple gravity-operated flush system, and can be repaired easily using the directions on the following pages. Some one-piece toilets use a complicated, high-pressure flush valve. Repairing these toilets can be difficult, so this work should be left to a professional.

Problems	Repairs
Toilet handle sticks, or is hard to push.	1. Adjust lift wires (page 74). 2. Clean & adjust handle (page 74).
Handle is loose.	1. Adjust handle (page 74). 2. Reattach lift chain or lift wires to lever (page 74).
Toilet will not flush at all.	1. Make sure water is turned on. 2. Adjust lift chain or lift wires (page 74).
Toilet does not flush completely.	1. Adjust lift chain (page 74). 2. Adjust water level in tank (page 76).
Toilet overflows, or flushes sluggishly.	1. Clear clogged toilet (page 90). 2. Clear clogged main waste and vent stack (page 97).
Toilet runs continuously.	1. Adjust lift wires or lift chain (page 74). 2. Replace leaky float ball (page 75). 3. Adjust water level in tank (page 76). 4. Adjust & clean flush valve (page 79). 5. Replace flush valve (page 79). 6. Repair or replace ballcock (pages 77 to 78).
Water on floor around toilet.	1. Tighten tank bolts and water connections (page 80). 2. Insulate tank to prevent condensation (page 80). 3. Replace wax ring (pages 81 to 82). 4. Replace cracked tank or bowl (pages 80 to 83).

Making Minor Adjustments

Many common toilet problems can be fixed by making minor adjustments to the handle and the attached lift chain (or lift wires).

If the handle sticks or is hard to push, remove the tank cover and clean the handle mounting nut. Make sure the lift wires are straight.

If the toilet will not flush completely unless the handle is held down, you may need to remove excess slack in the lift chain.

If the toilet will not flush at all, the lift chain may be broken or may need to be reattached to the handle lever.

A continuously running toilet (page opposite) can be caused by bent lift wires, kinks in a lift chain, or lime buildup on the handle mounting nut. Clean and adjust the handle and the lift wires or chain to fix the problem.

Everything You Need:

Tools: adjustable wrench, needlenose pliers, screwdriver, small wire brush.

Materials: vinegar.

How to Adjust a Toilet Handle & Lift Chain (or Lift Wires)

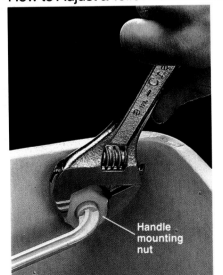

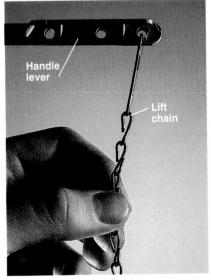

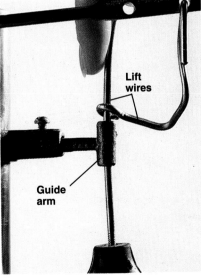

Clean and adjust handle mounting nut so handle operates smoothly. Mounting nut has reversed threads. Loosen nut by turning clockwise; tighten by turning counterclockwise. Remove lime buildup by scrubbing handle parts with a brush dipped in vinegar.

Adjust lift chain so it hangs straight from handle lever, with about ½" of slack. Remove excess slack in chain by hooking the chain in a different hole in the handle lever, or by removing links with needlenose pliers. A broken lift chain must be replaced.

Adjust lift wires (found on toilets without lift chains) so that wires are straight and operate smoothly when handle is pushed. A sticky handle often can be fixed by straightening bent lift wires.

Fixing a Running Toilet

The sound of continuously running water occurs if fresh water continues to enter the toilet tank after the flush cycle is complete. A running toilet can waste 20 or more gallons of fresh water each day.

To fix a running toilet, first jiggle the toilet handle. If the sound of running water stops, then either the handle or the lift wires (or lift chain) need to be adjusted (page opposite).

If the sound of running water does not stop when the handle is jiggled, then remove the tank cover and check to see if the float ball is touching the side of the tank. If necessary, bend the float arm to reposition the float ball away from the side of the tank. Make sure the float ball is not leaking. To check for leaks, unscrew the float ball and shake it gently. If there is water inside the ball, replace it.

If these minor adjustments do not fix the problem, then you will need to adjust or repair the ballcock or the flush valve (photo, right). Follow the directions on the following pages.

Everything You Need:

Tools: screwdriver, small wire brush, sponge, adjustable wrenches, spud wrench or channel-type pliers.

Materials: universal washer kit, ballcock (if needed), ballcock seals, emery cloth, Scotch Brite® pad, flapper or tank ball, flush valve (if needed).

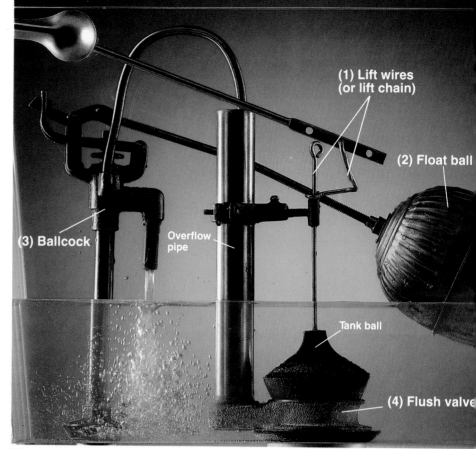

(1) Lift wires (or lift chain)

(2) Float ball

(3) Ballcock

Overflow pipe

Tank ball

(4) Flush valve

The sound of continuously running water can be caused by several different problems: if the **lift wire (1)** (or lift chain) is bent or kinked; if the **float ball (2)** leaks or rubs against the side of the tank; if a faulty **ballcock (3)** does not shut off the fresh water supply; or if the **flush valve (4)** allows water to leak down into the toilet bowl. First, check the lift wires and float ball. If making simple adjustments and repairs to these parts does not fix the problem, then you will need to repair the ballcock or flush valve (photo, below).

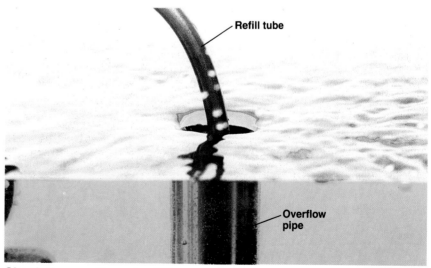

Refill tube

Overflow pipe

Check the overflow pipe if the sound of running water continues after the float ball and lift wires are adjusted. If you see **water flowing into the overflow pipe,** the ballcock needs to be repaired. First, adjust ballcock to lower the water level in the tank (page 76). If problem continues, repair or replace the ballcock (pages 77 to 78). If **water is not flowing into the overflow pipe,** then the flush valve needs to be repaired (page 79). First check the tank ball (or flapper) for wear, and replace if necessary. If problem continues, replace the flush valve.

How to Adjust a Ballcock to Set Water Level

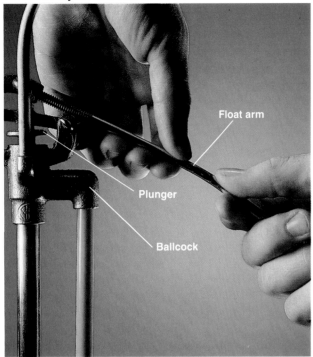

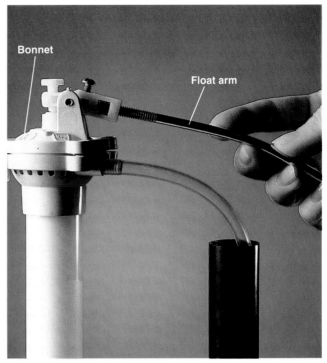

Traditional plunger-valve ballcock is made of brass. Water flow is controlled by a plunger attached to the float arm and ball. Lower the water level by bending the float arm downward slightly. Raise the water level by bending float arm upward.

Diaphragm ballcock usually is made of plastic, and has a wide bonnet that contains a rubber diaphragm. Lower the water level by bending the float arm downward slightly. Raise the water level by bending float arm upward.

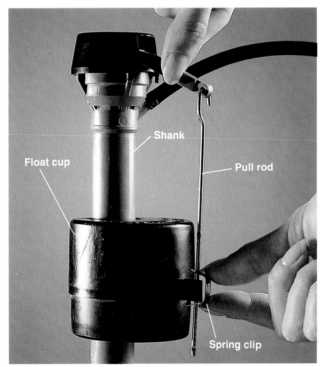

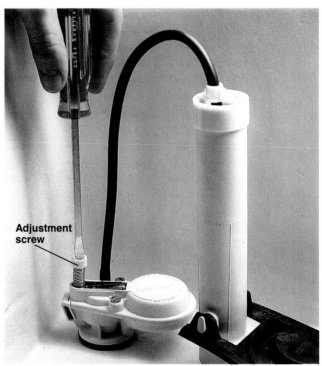

Float cup ballcock is made of plastic, and is easy to adjust. Lower the water level by pinching spring clip on pull rod, and moving float cup downward on the ballcock shank. Raise the water level by moving the cup upward.

Floatless ballcock controls water level with a pressure-sensing device. Lower the water level by turning the adjustment screw counterclockwise, ½ turn at a time. Raise water level by turning screw clockwise. Floatless ballcocks are repair-free, but eventually may need to be replaced.

How to Repair a Plunger-valve Ballcock

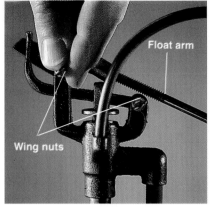

1 Shut off the water, and flush to empty the tank. Remove the wing nuts on the ballcock. Slip out the float arm.

2 Pull up on plunger to remove it. Pry out packing washer or O-ring. Pry out plunger washer. (Remove stem screw, if necessary.)

3 Install replacement washers. Clean sediment from inside of ballcock with a wire brush. Re-assemble ballcock.

How to Repair a Diaphragm Ballcock

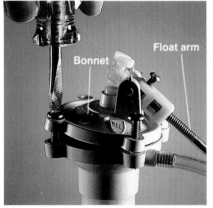

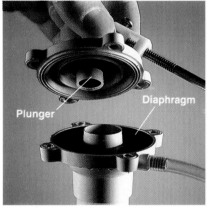

1 Shut off the water, and flush to empty the tank. Remove the screws from the bonnet.

2 Lift off float arm with bonnet attached. Check diaphragm and plunger for wear.

3 Replace any stiff or cracked parts. If assembly is badly worn, replace the entire ballcock (page 78).

How to Repair a Float Cup Ballcock

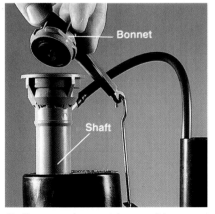

1 Shut off the water, and flush to empty the tank. Remove the ballcock cap.

2 Remove bonnet by pushing down on shaft and turning counterclockwise. Clean out sediment inside ballcock with wire brush.

3 Replace the seal. If assembly is badly worn, replace the entire ballcock (page 78).

How to Install a New Ballcock

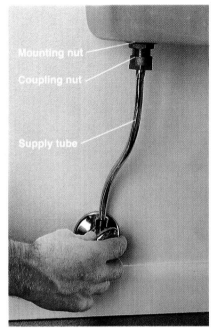

1 Shut off water, and flush toilet to empty tank. Use a sponge to remove remaining water. Disconnect supply tube coupling nut and ballcock mounting nut with adjustable wrench. Remove old ballcock.

2 Attach cone washer to new ballcock tailpiece and insert tailpiece into tank opening.

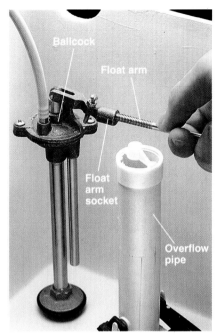

3 Align the float arm socket so that float arm will pass behind overflow pipe. Screw float arm onto ballcock. Screw float ball onto float arm.

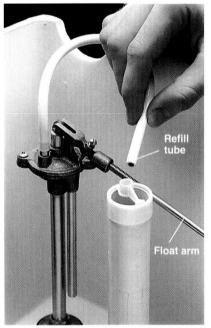

4 Bend or clip refill tube so tip is inside overflow pipe.

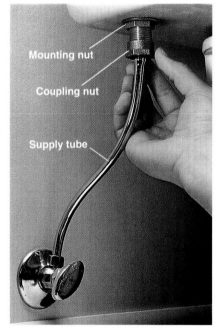

5 Screw mounting nut and supply tube coupling nut onto ballcock tailpiece, and tighten with an adjustable wrench. Turn on the water, and check for leaks.

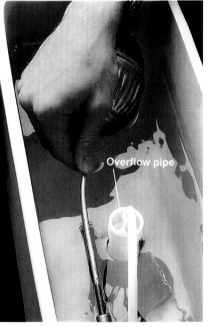

6 Adjust the water level in the tank so it is about ½" below top of the overflow pipe (page 76).

How to Adjust & Clean a Flush Valve

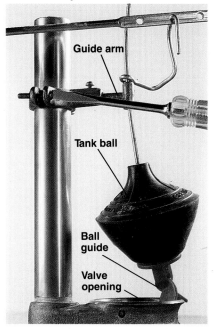

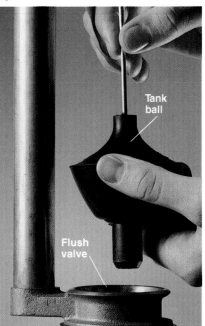

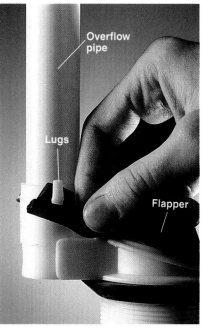

Adjust tank ball (or flapper) so it is directly over flush valve. Tank ball has a guide arm that can be loosened so that tank ball can be repositioned. (Some tank balls have a ball guide that helps seat the tank ball into the flush valve.)

Replace the tank ball if it is cracked or worn. Tank balls have a threaded fitting that screws onto the lift wire. Clean opening of the flush valve, using emery cloth (for brass valves) or a Scotch Brite® pad (for plastic valves).

Replace flapper if it is worn. Flappers are attached to small lugs on the sides of overflow pipe.

How to Install a New Flush Valve

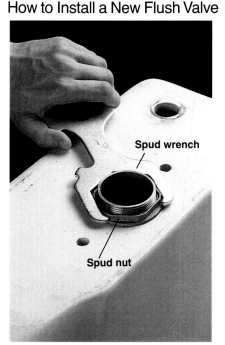

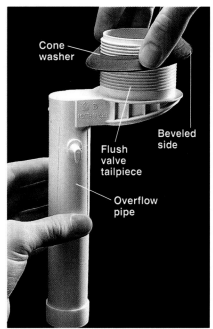

1 Shut off water, disconnect ballcock (page opposite, step 1), and remove toilet tank (page 81, steps 1 and 2). Remove old flush valve by unscrewing spud nut with spud wrench or channel-type pliers.

2 Slide cone washer onto tailpiece of new flush valve. Beveled side of cone washer should face end of tailpiece. Insert flush valve into tank opening so that overflow pipe faces ballcock.

3 Screw spud nut onto tailpiece of flush valve, and tighten with a spud wrench or channel-type pliers. Place soft spud washer over tailpiece, and reinstall toilet tank (pages 82 to 83).

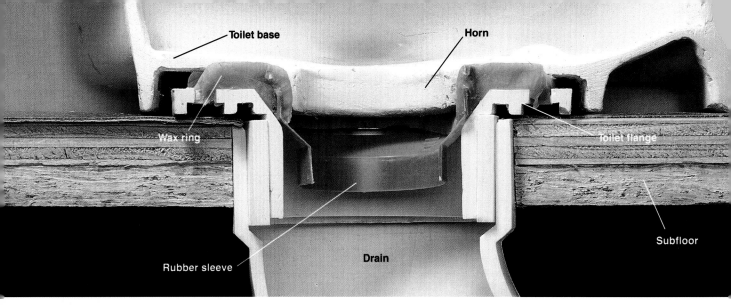

Toilet base · Horn · Wax ring · Toilet flange · Rubber sleeve · Drain · Subfloor

Fixing a Leaking Toilet

Water leaking onto the floor around a toilet may be caused by several different problems. The leaking must be fixed as soon as possible to prevent moisture from damaging the subfloor.

First, make sure all connections are tight. If moisture drips from the tank during humid weather, it is probably condensation. Fix this "sweating" problem by insulating the inside of the tank with foam panels. A crack in a toilet tank also can cause leaks. A cracked tank must be replaced.

Water seeping around the base of a toilet can be caused by an old wax ring that no longer seals against the drain (photo, above), or by a cracked toilet base. If leaking occurs during or just after a flush, replace the wax ring. If leaking is constant, the toilet base is cracked and must be replaced.

New toilets sometimes are sold with flush valves and ballcocks already installed. If these parts are not included, you will need to purchase them. When buying a new toilet, consider a water-saver design. Water-saver toilets use less than half the water needed by a standard toilet.

Everything You Need:

Tools: sponge, adjustable wrench, putty knife, ratchet wrench, screwdriver.

Materials: tank liner kit, abrasive cleanser, rag, wax ring, plumber's putty. *For new installation:* new toilet, toilet handle, ballcock, flush valve, tank bolts, toilet seat.

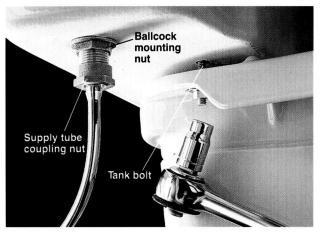

Tighten all connections slightly. Tighten nuts on tank bolts with a ratchet wrench. Tighten ballcock mounting nut and supply tube coupling nut with an adjustable wrench. **Caution: overtightening tank bolts may crack the toilet tank.**

Insulate toilet tank to prevent "sweating," using a toilet liner kit. First, shut off water, drain tank, and clean inside of tank with abrasive cleanser. Cut plastic foam panels to fit bottom, sides, front, and back of tank. Attach panels to tank with adhesive (included in kit). Let adhesive cure as directed.

How to Remove & Replace a Wax Ring & Toilet

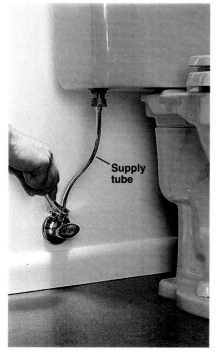

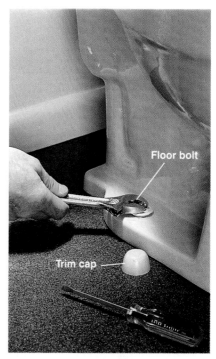

1 Turn off water, and flush to empty toilet tank. Use a sponge to remove remaining water in tank and bowl. Disconnect supply tube with an adjustable wrench.

2 Remove the nuts from the tank bolts with a ratchet wrench. Carefully remove the tank and set it aside.

3 Pry off the floor bolt trim caps at the base of the toilet. Remove the floor nuts with an adjustable wrench.

4 Straddle the toilet and rock the bowl from side to side until the seal breaks. Carefully lift the toilet off the floor bolts and set it on its side. Small amount of water may spill from the toilet trap.

5 Remove old wax from the toilet flange in the floor. Plug the drain opening with a damp rag to prevent sewer gases from rising into the house.

6 If old toilet will be reused, clean old wax and putty from the horn and the base of the toilet.

(continued next page)

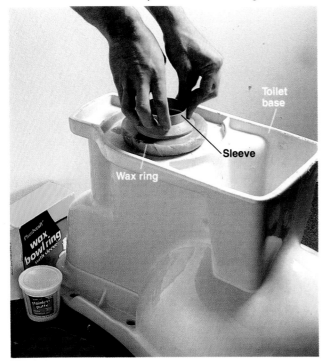

7 Turn stool upside down. Place new wax ring over drain horn. If ring has a rubber or plastic sleeve, sleeve should face away from toilet. Apply a bead of plumber's putty to bottom edge of toilet base.

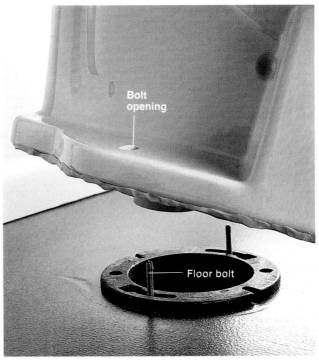

8 Position the toilet over drain so that the floor bolts fit through openings in base of toilet. Thread washers and nuts onto floor bolts, and tighten with adjustable wrench until snug.

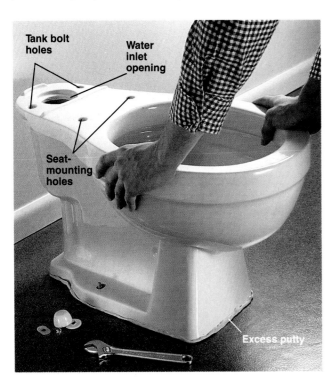

9 Press down on toilet base to compress wax and putty. Retighten floor nuts until snug. **Caution: over-tightening nuts may crack the base.** Wipe away excess plumber's putty. Cover nuts with trim caps.

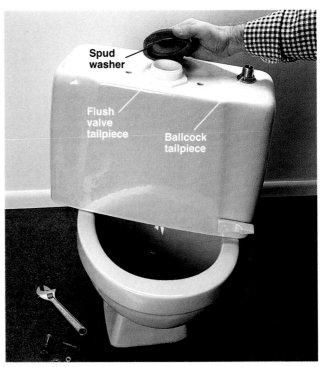

10 Prepare tank for installation. If necessary, install a handle (page 74), ballcock (page 78), and flush valve (page 79). Carefully turn tank upside down, and place soft spud washer over the flush valve tailpiece.

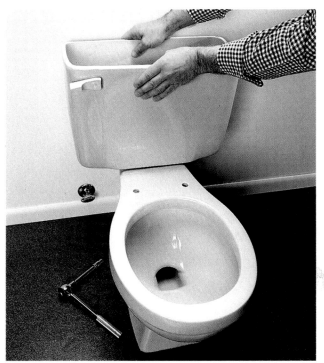

11 Turn tank right side up and position it on rear of toilet base so that spud washer is centered in water inlet opening.

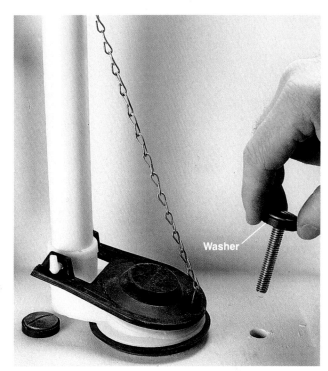

Washer

12 Line up the tank bolt holes with holes in base of toilet. Slide rubber washers onto the tank bolts and place the bolts through holes. From underneath the tank, thread washers and nuts onto the bolts.

13 Tighten nuts with ratchet wrench until tank is snug. Use caution when tightening nuts: most toilet tanks rest on the spud washer, not directly on the toilet base.

14 Attach the water supply tube to the ballcock tailpiece with an adjustable wrench (page 78). Turn on the water and test toilet. Tighten tank bolts and water connections, if necessary.

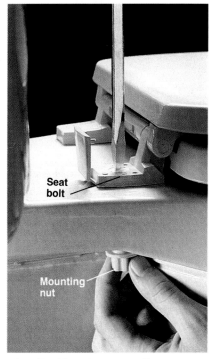

Seat bolt

Mounting nut

15 Position the new toilet seat, if needed, inserting seat bolts into mounting holes in toilet. Screw mounting nuts onto the seat bolts, and tighten.

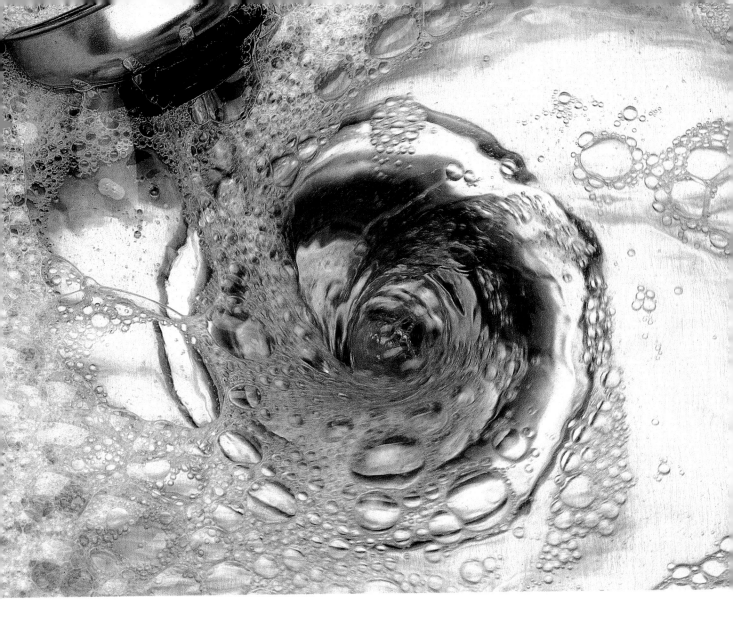

Clearing Clogs & Fixing Drains

Clear a clogged drain with a plunger, hand auger, or blow bag. A plunger breaks up clogs by forcing air pressure into the drain line. Because a plunger is effective and simple to use, it should be the first choice for clearing a clog.

A hand auger has a flexible steel cable that is pushed into the drain line to break up or remove obstructions. An auger is easy to use, but for best results the user must know the "feel" of the cable in the drain line. A little experience often is necessary to tell the difference between a soap clog and a bend in the drain line (pages 88 to 89).

A blow bag hooks to a garden hose and uses water pressure to clear clogs. Blow bags are most effective on clogs in floor drains (page 95).

Use caustic, acid-based chemical drain cleaners only as a last resort. These drain cleaners, usually available at hardware stores and supermarkets, will dissolve clogs, but they also may damage pipes and must be handled with caution. Always read the manufacturer's directions completely.

Regular maintenance helps keep drains working properly. Flush drains once each week with hot tap water to keep them free of soap, grease, and debris. Or, treat drains once every six months with a non-caustic (copper sulfide- or sodium hydroxide-based) drain cleaner. A non-caustic cleaner will not harm pipes.

Occasionally, leaks may occur in the drain lines or around the drain opening. Most leaks in drain lines are fixed easily by gently tightening all pipe connections. If the leak is at the sink drain opening, fix or replace the strainer body assembly (page 87).

Clearing Clogged Sinks

Every sink has a drain trap and a fixture drain line. Sink clogs usually are caused by a buildup of soap and hair in the trap or fixture drain line. Remove clogs by using a plunger, disconnecting and cleaning the trap (page 86), or using a hand auger (pages 88 to 89).

Many sinks hold water with a mechanical plug called a *pop-up stopper*. If the sink will not hold standing water, or if water in the sink drains too slowly, the pop-up stopper must be cleaned and adjusted (page 86).

Everything You Need:

Tools: plunger, channel-type pliers, small wire brush, screwdriver.

Materials: rag, bucket, replacement gaskets.

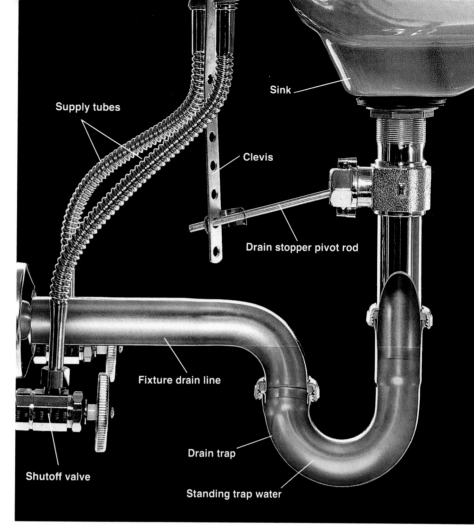

Drain trap holds water that seals the drain line and prevents sewer gases from entering the home. Each time a drain is used, the standing trap water is flushed away and replaced by new water. The shape of the trap and fixture drain line may resemble the letter "P," and sink traps sometimes are called P-traps.

How to Clear Sink Drains with a Plunger

1 Remove drain stopper. Some pop-up stoppers lift out directly; others turn counterclockwise. On some older types of stoppers, the pivot rod must be removed to free the stopper.

2 Stuff a wet rag in sink overflow opening. Rag prevents air from breaking the suction of the plunger. Place plunger cup over drain and run enough water to cover the rubber cup. Move plunger handle up and down rapidly to break up the clog.

How to Clean & Adjust a Pop-up Sink Drain Stopper

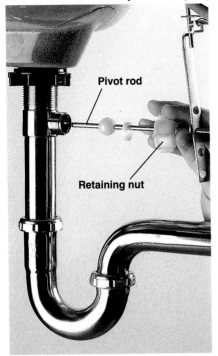

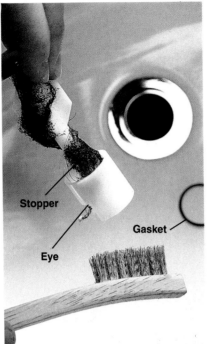

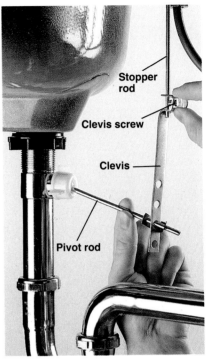

1 Raise stopper lever to full upright (closed) position. Unscrew the retaining nut that holds pivot rod in position. Pull pivot rod out of drain pipe to release stopper.

2 Remove stopper. Clean debris from stopper, using a small wire brush. Inspect gasket for wear or damage, and replace if necessary. Reinstall stopper.

3 If sink does not drain properly, adjust clevis. Loosen clevis screw. Slide clevis up or down on stopper rod to adjust position of stopper. Tighten clevis screw.

How to Remove & Clean a Sink Drain Trap

1 Place bucket under trap to catch water and debris. Loosen slip nuts on trap bend with channel-type pliers. Unscrew nuts by hand and slide away from connections. Pull off trap bend.

2 Dump out debris. Clean trap bend with a small wire brush. Inspect slip nut washers for wear, and replace if necessary. Reinstall trap bend, and tighten slip nuts.

Fixing Leaky Sink Strainers

A leak under a sink may be caused by a strainer body that is not properly sealed to the sink drain opening. To check for leaks, close the drain stopper and fill sink with water. From underneath sink, inspect the strainer assembly for leaks.

Remove the strainer body, clean it, and replace the gaskets and plumber's putty. Or, replace the strainer with a new one, available at home centers.

Everything You Need:

Tools: channel-type pliers, spud wrench, hammer, putty knife.

Materials: plumber's putty, replacement parts (if needed).

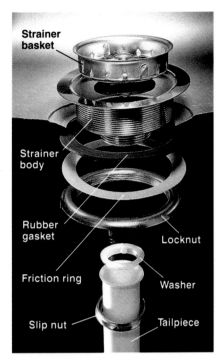

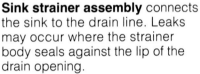

Sink strainer assembly connects the sink to the drain line. Leaks may occur where the strainer body seals against the lip of the drain opening.

1 Unscrew slip nuts from both ends of tailpiece, using channel-type pliers. Disconnect tailpiece from strainer body and trap bend. Remove tailpiece.

2 Remove the locknut, using a spud wrench. Stubborn locknuts may be removed by tapping on the lugs with a hammer. Unscrew the locknut completely, and remove the strainer assembly.

3 Remove old putty from the drain opening, using a putty knife. If reusing the old strainer body, clean off old putty from under the flange. Old gaskets and washers should be replaced.

4 Apply a bead of plumber's putty to the lip of the drain opening. Press strainer body into drain opening. From under the sink, place rubber gasket, then metal or fiber friction ring, over strainer. Reinstall locknut and tighten. Reinstall tailpiece.

How to Clear a Fixture Drain Line with a Hand Auger

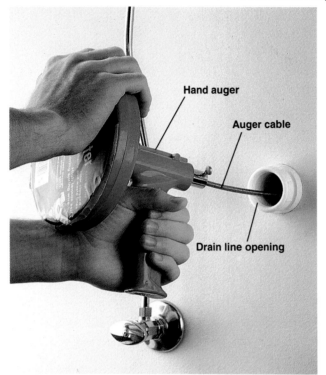

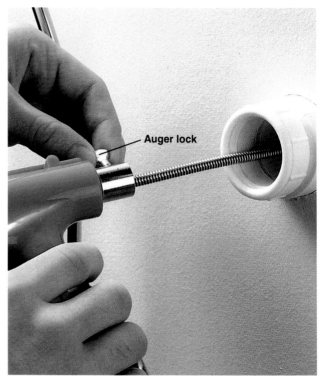

1 Remove trap bend (page 86). Push the end of the auger cable into the drain line opening until resistance is met. This resistance usually indicates end of cable has reached a bend in the drain pipe.

2 Set the auger lock so that at least 6" of cable extends out of the opening. Crank the auger handle in a clockwise direction to move the end of the cable past bend in drain line.

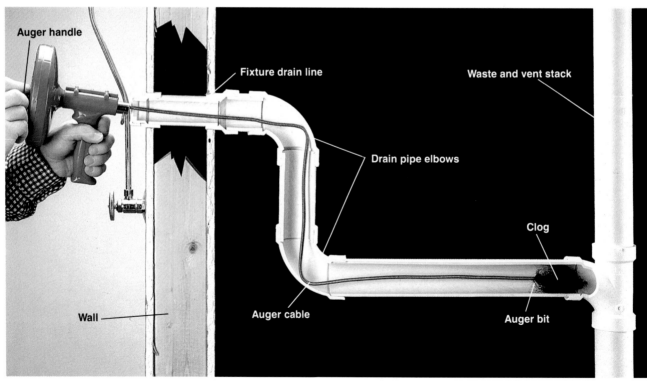

3 Release the lock and continue pushing the cable into the opening until firm resistance is felt. Set the auger lock and crank the handle in a clockwise direction. Solid resistance that prevents the cable from advancing indicates a clog. Some clogs, such as a sponge or an accumulation of hair, can be snagged and retrieved (step 4). Continuous resistance that allows the cable to advance slowly is probably a soap clog (step 5).

Hand grip

4 Pull an obstruction out of the line by releasing the auger lock and cranking the handle clockwise. If no object can be retrieved, reconnect the trap bend and use the auger to clear the nearest branch drain line or main waste and vent stack (pages 96 to 97).

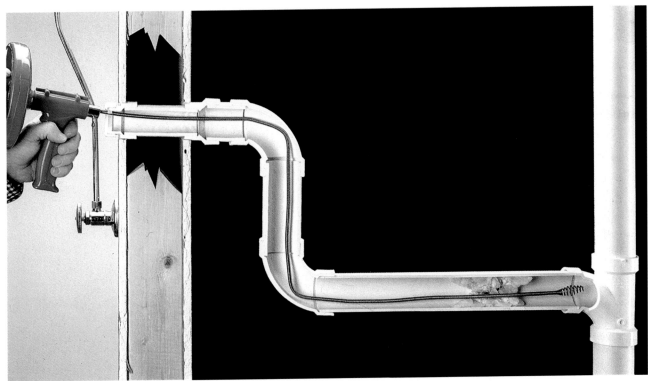

5 Continuous resistance indicates a soap clog. Bore through the clog by cranking the auger handle clockwise while applying steady pressure on the hand grip of the auger. Repeat the procedure two or three times, then retrieve the cable. Reconnect the trap bend and flush the system with hot tap water to remove debris.

Clearing Clogged Toilets

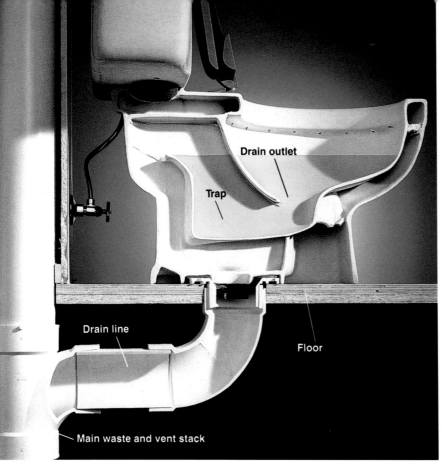

Most toilet clogs occur because an object is stuck inside the toilet trap. Use a flanged plunger or a closet auger to remove the clog.

A toilet that is sluggish during the flush cycle may be partially blocked. Clear the blockage with a plunger or closet auger. Occasionally, a sluggish toilet flush indicates a blocked waste and vent stack. Clear the stack as shown on page 97.

Everything You Need:

Tools: flanged plunger, closet auger.

Materials: bucket.

Toilet drain system has a drain outlet at the bottom of the bowl and a built-in trap. The toilet drain is connected to a drain line and a main waste and vent stack.

How to Clear a Toilet with a Plunger

Place cup of flanged plunger over drain outlet opening. Plunge up and down rapidly. Slowly pour a bucket of water into bowl to flush debris through drain. If toilet does not drain, repeat plunging, or clear clog with a closet auger.

How to Clear a Toilet with a Closet Auger

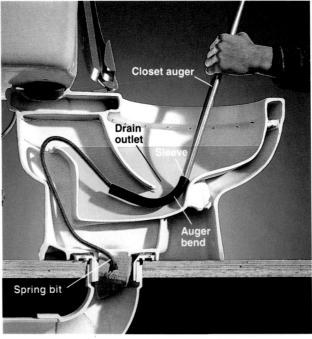

Place the auger bend in the bottom of the drain opening, and push the auger cable into the trap. Crank the auger handle in a clockwise direction to snag obstruction. Continue cranking while retrieving the cable to pull the obstruction out of the trap.

Clearing Clogged Shower Drains

Shower drain clogs usually are caused by an accumulation of hair in the drain line. Remove the strainer cover and look for clogs in the drain opening (below). Some clogs are removed easily with a piece of stiff wire.

Stubborn clogs should be removed with a plunger or hand auger.

Everything You Need:

Tools: screwdriver, flashlight, plunger, hand auger.

Materials: stiff wire.

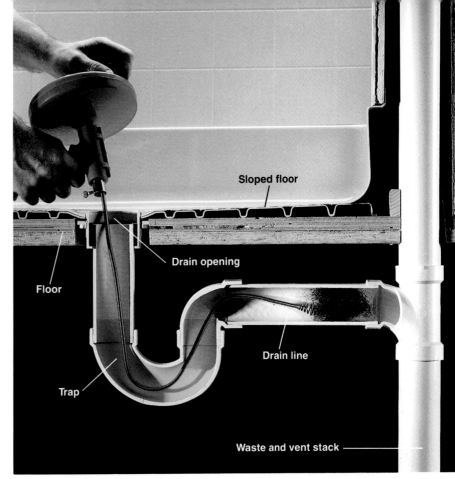

Shower drain system has a sloped floor, a drain opening, a trap, and a drain line that connects to a branch drain line or waste and vent stack.

How to Clear a Shower Drain

Check for clogs. Remove strainer cover, using a screwdriver. Use a flashlight to look for hair clogs in the drain opening. Use a stiff wire to clear shower drain of hair or to snag any obstructions.

Use a plunger to clear most shower drain clogs. Place the rubber cup over the drain opening. Pour enough water into the shower stall to cover the lip of the cup. Move plunger handle up and down rapidly.

Clear stubborn clogs in the shower drain with a hand auger. Use the auger as shown on pages 88 to 89.

91

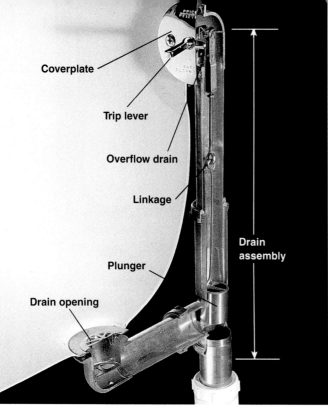

Coverplate

Trip lever

Overflow drain

Linkage

Plunger

Drain opening

Drain assembly

Plunger-type tub drain has a hollow brass plug, called a *plunger*, that slides up and down inside the overflow drain to seal off the water flow. The plunger is moved by a trip lever and linkage that runs through the overflow drain.

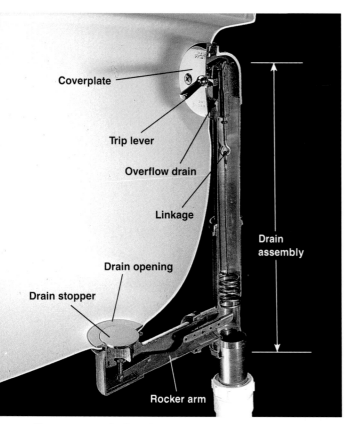

Coverplate

Trip lever

Overflow drain

Linkage

Drain opening

Drain assembly

Drain stopper

Rocker arm

Pop-up tub drain has a rocker arm that pivots to open or close a metal drain stopper. The rocker arm is moved by a trip lever and linkage that runs through the overflow drain.

Fixing Tub Drains

When water in the tub drains slowly or not at all, remove and inspect the drain assembly. Both plunger and pop-up type drain mechanisms catch hair and other debris that cause clogs.

If cleaning the drain assembly does not fix the problem, the tub drain line is clogged. Clear the line with a plunger or a hand auger. Always stuff a wet rag in the overflow drain opening before plunging the tub drain. The rag prevents air from breaking the suction of the plunger. When using an auger, always insert the cable down through the overflow drain opening.

If the tub will not hold water with the drain closed, or if the tub continues to drain slowly after the assembly has been cleaned, then the drain assembly needs adjustment. Remove the assembly, and follow the instructions on the opposite page.

Everything You Need:

Tools: plunger, screwdriver, small wire brush, needlenose pliers, hand auger.

Materials: vinegar, heatproof grease, rag.

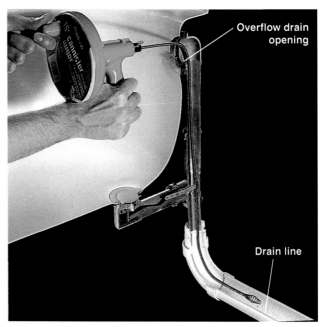

Overflow drain opening

Drain line

Clear a tub drain by running the auger cable through the overflow opening. First, remove the coverplate and carefully lift out the drain linkage (page opposite). Push auger cable into the opening until resistance is felt (pages 88 to 89). After using the auger, replace drain linkage. Open drain and run hot water through drain to flush out any debris.

How to Clean & Adjust a Plunger-type Tub Drain

1 Remove screws on coverplate. Carefully pull coverplate, linkage, and plunger from the overflow drain opening.

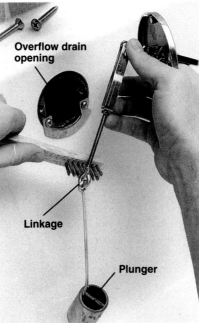

2 Clean linkage and plunger with a small wire brush dipped in vinegar. Lubricate assembly with heat-proof grease.

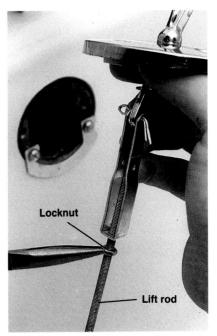

3 Adjust drain flow and fix leaks by adjusting linkage. Unscrew locknut on threaded lift rod, using needlenose pliers. Screw rod down about ⅛". Tighten locknut and re-install entire assembly.

How to Clean & Adjust a Pop-up Tub Drain

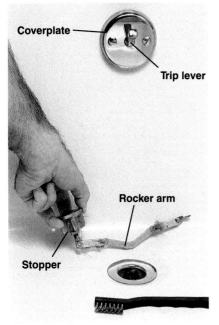

1 Raise trip lever to the full open position. Carefully pull stopper and rocker arm assembly from drain opening. Clean hair or debris from rocker arm with a small wire brush.

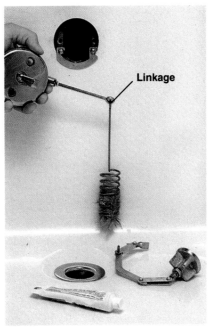

2 Remove screws from coverplate. Pull coverplate, trip lever, and linkage from overflow drain. Remove hair and debris. Remove corrosion with a small wire brush dipped in vinegar. Lubricate linkage with heat-proof grease.

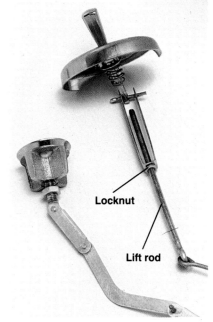

3 Adjust drain flow and fix leaks by adjusting the linkage. Loosen locknut on threaded lift rod and screw lift rod up about ⅛". Tighten locknut and reinstall entire assembly.

Cover

Line in from tub

Line in from sink

Line out to toilet drain line

Clearing Clogged Drum Traps

In older homes, clogs in bathroom sinks or bathtubs may be caused by blockage in the drain lines connected to a drum trap. Remove the drum trap cover and use a hand auger to clear each drain line.

Drum traps usually are located in the floor next to the bathtub. They are identified by a flat, screw-in type cover or plug that is flush with the floor. Occasionally, a drum trap may be located under the floor. This type of drum trap will be positioned upside down so that the plug is accessible from below.

Everything You Need:

Tools: adjustable wrench, hand auger.

Materials: rags or towels, penetrating oil, Teflon™ tape.

A drum trap is a canister made of lead or cast iron. Usually, more than one fixture drain line is connected to the drum. Drum traps are not vented, and they are no longer approved for new plumbing installations.

How to Clear a Clogged Drum Trap

1 Place rags or towels around the opening of the drum trap to absorb water that may be backed up in the lines.

2 Remove the trap cover, using an adjustable wrench. Work carefully: older drum traps may be made of lead, which gets brittle with age. If cover does not unscrew easily, apply penetrating oil to lubricate the threads.

3 Use a hand auger (pages 88 to 89) to clear each drain line. Then wrap the threads of the cover with Teflon™ tape and install. Flush all drains with hot water for five minutes.

Clearing Clogged Floor Drains

When water backs up onto a basement floor, there is a clog in either the floor drain line, drain trap, or the sewer service line. Clogs in the drain line or trap may be cleared with a hand auger or a blow bag. To clear a sewer service line, see page 96.

Blow bags are especially useful for clearing clogs in floor drain lines. A blow bag attaches to a garden hose and is inserted directly into the floor drain line. The bag fills with water and then releases a powerful spurt that dislodges clogs.

Everything You Need:

Tools: adjustable wrench, screwdriver, hand auger, blow bag.

Materials: garden hose.

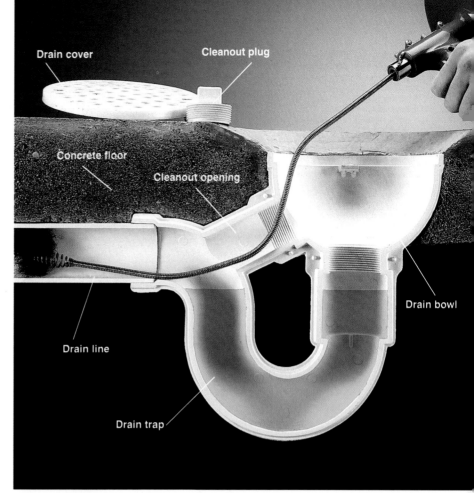

Clear clogged floor drains using a hand auger. Remove the drain cover, then use a wrench to unscrew the cleanout plug in the drain bowl. Push the auger cable through the cleanout opening directly into the drain line.

How to Use a Blow Bag to Clear a Floor Drain

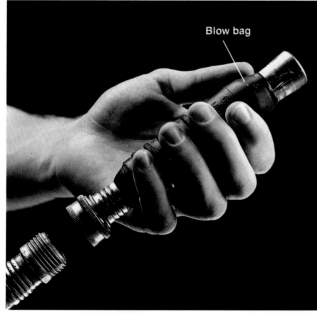

1 Attach blow bag to garden hose, then attach hose to a hose bib or utility faucet.

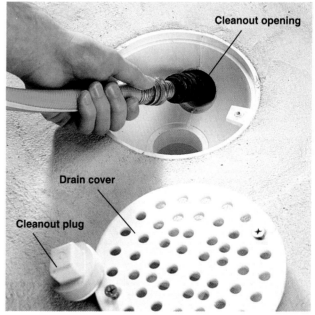

2 Remove drain cover and cleanout plug. Insert the blow bag completely into the cleanout opening and turn on water. Allow several minutes for the blow bag to work properly.

Clearing Clogs in Branch & Main Drain Lines

If using a plunger or a hand auger does not clear a clog in a fixture drain line, it means that the blockage may be in a branch drain line, the main waste and vent stack, or the sewer service line (see the photo on page 7).

First, use an auger to clear the branch drain line closest to any stopped-up fixtures. Branch drain lines may be serviced through the cleanout fittings located at the end of the branch. Because waste water may be backed up in the drain lines, always open a cleanout with caution. Place a bucket and rags under the opening to catch waste water. Never position yourself directly under a cleanout opening while unscrewing the plug or cover.

If using an auger on the branch line does not solve the problem, then the clog may be located in a main waste and vent stack. To clear the stack, run an auger cable down through the roof vent. Make sure that the cable of your auger is long enough to reach down the entire length of the stack. If it is not, you may want to rent or borrow another auger. Always use extreme caution when working on a ladder or on a roof.

If no clog is present in the main stack, the problem may be located in the sewer service line. Locate the main cleanout, usually a Y-shaped fitting at the bottom of the main waste and vent stack. Remove the plug and push the cable of a hand auger into the opening.

Some sewer service lines in older homes have a house trap. The house trap is a U-shaped fitting located at the point where the sewer line exits the house. Most of the fitting will be beneath the floor surface, but it can be identified by its two openings. Use a hand auger to clean a house trap.

If the auger meets solid resistance in the sewer line, retrieve the cable and inspect the bit. Fine, hair-like roots on the bit indicate the line is clogged with tree roots. Dirt on the bit indicates a collapsed line.

Use a power auger to clear sewer service lines that are clogged with tree roots. Power augers (page 13) are available at rental centers. However, a power auger is a large, heavy piece of equipment. Before renting, consider the cost of rental and the level of your do-it-yourself skills versus the price of a professional sewer cleaning service. If you rent a power auger, ask the rental dealer for complete instructions on how to operate the equipment.

Always consult a professional sewer cleaning service if you suspect a collapsed line.

Everything You Need:

Tools: adjustable wrench or pipe wrench, hand auger, cold chisel, ball peen hammer.

Materials: bucket, rags, penetrating oil, cleanout plug (if needed), pipe joint compound.

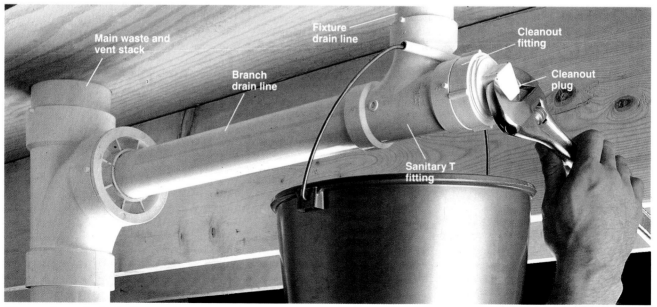

Clear a branch drain line by locating the cleanout fitting at the end of the line. Place a bucket underneath the opening to catch waste water, then slowly unscrew the cleanout plug with an adjustable wrench. Clear clogs in the branch drain line with a hand auger (pages 88 to 89).

Clear the main waste and vent stack by running the cable of a hand auger down through the roof vent. Always use extreme caution while working on a ladder or roof.

Clear the house trap in a sewer service line using a hand auger. Slowly remove only the plug on the "street side" of the trap. If water seeps out the opening as the plug is removed, the clog is in the sewer line beyond the trap. If no water seeps out, auger the trap. If no clog is present in the trap, replace the street-side plug and remove the house-side plug. Use the auger to clear clogs located between the house trap and main stack.

How to Remove & Replace a Main Drain Cleanout Plug

1 Remove the cleanout plug, using a large wrench. If plug does not turn out, apply penetrating oil around edge of plug, wait 10 minutes, and try again. Place rags and a bucket under fitting opening to catch any water that may be backed up in the line.

2 Remove stubborn plugs by placing the cutting edge of chisel on edge of plug. Strike chisel with a ball peen hammer to move plug counterclockwise. If plug does not turn out, break it into pieces with the chisel and hammer. Remove all broken pieces.

3 Replace old plug with new plastic plug. Apply pipe joint compound to the threads of the replacement plug and screw into cleanout fitting.

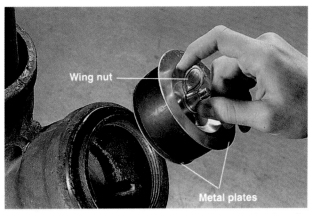

Alternate: Replace old plug with an expandable rubber plug. A wing nut squeezes the rubber core between two metal plates. The rubber bulges slightly to create a watertight seal.

Tub & Shower Plumbing

Tub and shower faucets have the same basic designs as sink faucets, and the techniques for repairing leaks are the same as described in the faucet repair section of this book (pages 49 to 59). To identify your faucet design, you may need to take off the handle and disassemble the faucet.

When a tub and shower are combined, the shower head and the tub spout share the same hot and cold water supply lines and handles. Combination faucets are available as three-handle, two-handle,

Tub & Shower Combination Faucets

Shower head

Diverter valve

Hot water supply line

Cold water supply line

Tub spout

Three-handle faucet (pages 100 to 101) has valves that are either compression or cartridge design.

or single-handle types (below). The number of handles gives clues as to the design of the faucets and the kinds of repairs that may be necessary.

With combination faucets, a diverter valve or gate diverter is used to direct water flow to the tub spout or the shower head. On three-handle faucet types, the middle handle controls a diverter valve. If water does not shift easily from tub spout to shower head, or if water continues to run out the spout when the shower is on, the diverter valve probably needs to be cleaned and repaired (pages 100 to 101).

Two-handle and single-handle types use a gate diverter that is operated by a pull lever or knob on the tub spout. Although gate diverters rarely need repair, the lever occasionally may break, come

loose, or refuse to stay in the UP position. To repair a gate diverter set in a tub spout, replace the entire spout (page 103).

Tub and shower faucets and diverter valves may be set inside wall cavities. Removing them may require a deep-set ratchet wrench (pages 101, 103).

If spray from the shower head is uneven, clean the spray holes. If the shower head does not stay in an upright position, remove the head and replace the O-ring (page 106).

To add a shower to an existing tub, install a flexible shower adapter (page 107). Several manufacturers make complete conversion kits that allow a shower to be installed in less than one hour.

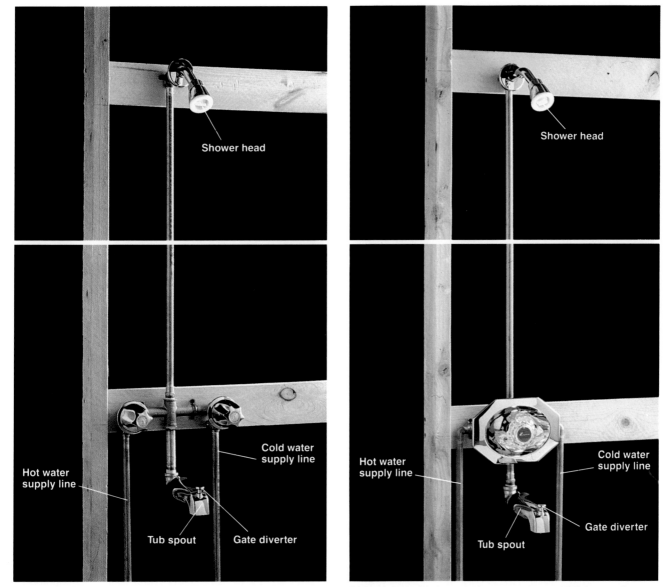

Two-handle faucet (pages 102 to 103) has valves that are either compression or cartridge design.

Single-handle faucet (pages 104 to 105) has valves that are cartridge, ball-type, or disc design.

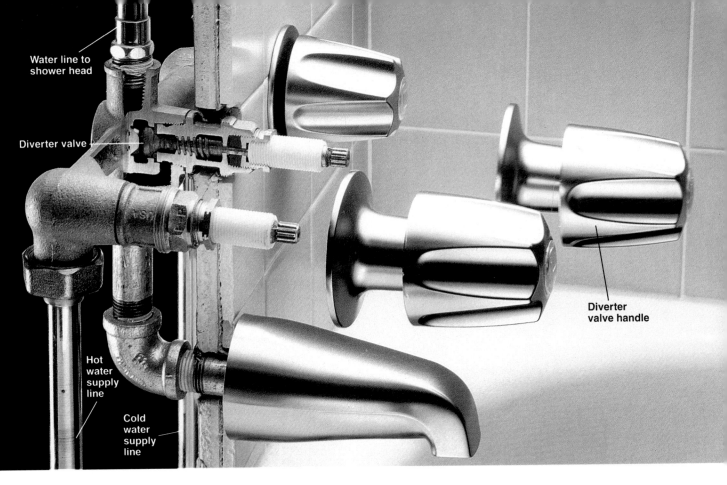

Water line to shower head

Diverter valve

Hot water supply line

Cold water supply line

Diverter valve handle

Fixing Three-handle Tub & Shower Faucets

A three-handle faucet type has handles to control hot and cold water, and a third handle that controls the diverter valve and directs water to either a tub spout or a shower head. The separate hot and cold handles indicate cartridge or compression faucet designs. To repair them, see pages 52 to 53 for cartridge, and 54 to 57 for compression.

If a diverter valve sticks, if water flow is weak, or if water runs out of the tub spout when the flow is directed to the shower head, the diverter needs to be repaired or replaced. Most diverter valves are similar to either compression or cartridge faucet valves. Compression type diverters can be repaired, but cartridge types should be replaced.

Remember to turn off the water (page 6) before beginning work.

Everything You Need:

Tools: screwdriver, adjustable wrench or channel-type pliers, deep-set ratchet wrench, small wire brush.

Materials: replacement diverter cartridge or universal washer kit, heatproof grease, vinegar.

How to Repair a Compression Diverter Valve

Escutcheon

Diverter valve handle

1 Remove the diverter valve handle with a screwdriver. Unscrew or pry off the escutcheon.

2 Remove bonnet nut with an adjustable wrench or channel-type pliers.

3 Unscrew the stem assembly, using a deep-set ratchet wrench. If necessary, chip away any mortar surrounding the bonnet nut (page 103, step 2).

Stem washer

Stem screw

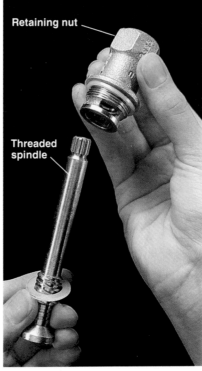

Retaining nut

Threaded spindle

4 Remove brass stem screw. Replace stem washer with an exact duplicate. If stem screw is worn, replace it.

5 Unscrew threaded spindle from retaining nut.

6 Clean sediment and lime build-up from nut, using a small wire brush dipped in vinegar. Coat all parts with heatproof grease and reassemble diverter valve.

Water line to
shower head

Bonnet
nut

Valve stem

Cold water
supply line

Diverter lever

Hot water
supply line

Gate diverter

Fixing Two-handle Tub & Shower Faucets

Two-handle tub and shower faucets are either cartridge or compression design. They may be repaired following the directions on pages 52 to 53 for cartridge, or pages 54 to 57 for compression. Because the valves of two-handle tub and shower faucets may be set inside the wall cavity, a deep-set socket wrench may be required to remove the valve stem.

Two-handle tub and shower designs have a gate diverter. A gate diverter is a simple mechanism located in the tub spout. A gate diverter closes the supply of water to the tub spout and redirects the flow to the shower head. Gate diverters seldom need repair. Occasionally, the lever may break, come loose, or refuse to stay in the UP position.

If the diverter fails to work properly, replace the tub spout. Tub spouts are inexpensive and easy to replace.

Remember to turn off the water (page 6) before beginning work.

Everything You Need:

Tools: screwdriver, allen wrench, pipe wrench, channel-type pliers, small cold chisel, ball peen hammer, deep-set ratchet wrench.

Materials: masking tape or cloth, pipe joint compound, replacement faucet parts as needed.

Tips on Replacing a Tub Spout

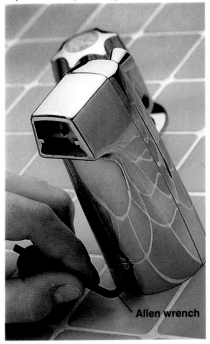

Check underneath tub spout for a small access slot. The slot indicates the spout is held in place with an allen screw. Remove the screw, using an allen wrench. Spout will slide off.

Unscrew faucet spout. Use a pipe wrench, or insert a large screwdriver or hammer handle into the spout opening and turn spout counterclockwise.

Spread pipe joint compound on threads of spout nipple before replacing spout.

How to Remove a Deep-set Faucet Valve

1 Remove handle, and unscrew the escutcheon with channel-type pliers. Pad the jaws of the pliers with masking tape to prevent scratching the escutcheon.

2 Chip away any mortar surrounding the bonnet nut, using a ball peen hammer and a small cold chisel.

3 Unscrew the bonnet nut with a deep-set ratchet wrench. Remove the bonnet nut and stem from the faucet body.

Water supply line
to shower head

Built-in shutoff valves

Hot water
supply line

Control valve

Cold water
supply line

Escutcheon

Gate diverter

Fixing Single-handle Tub & Shower Faucets

A single-handle tub and shower faucet has one valve that controls both water flow and temperature. Single-handle faucets may be ball-type, cartridge, or disc designs.

If a single-handle control valve leaks or does not function properly, disassemble the faucet, clean the valve, and replace any worn parts. Use the repair techniques described on pages 50 to 51 for ball-type, or pages 58 to 59 for ceramic disc. Repairing a single-handle cartridge faucet is shown on the opposite page.

Direction of the water flow to either the tub spout or the shower head is controlled by a gate diverter.

Gate diverters seldom need repair. Occasionally, the lever may break, come loose, or refuse to stay in the UP position. If the diverter fails to work properly, replace the tub spout (page 103).

Everything You Need:

Tools: screwdriver, adjustable wrench, channel-type pliers.

Materials: replacement parts as needed.

How to Repair a Single-handle Cartridge Tub & Shower Faucet

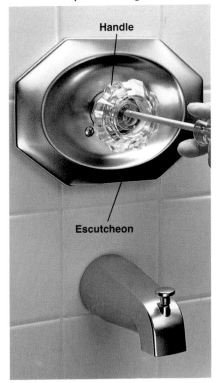

1 Use a screwdriver to remove the handle and escutcheon.

2 Turn off water supply at built-in shutoff valves or main shutoff valve (page 6).

3 Unscrew and remove retaining ring or bonnet nut, using an adjustable wrench.

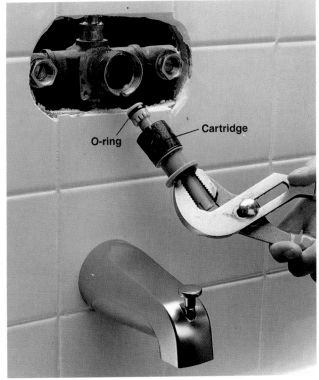

4 Remove cartridge assembly by grasping end of valve with channel-type pliers and pulling gently.

5 Flush valve body with clean water to remove sediment. Replace any worn O-rings. Reinstall cartridge and test valve. If faucet fails to work properly, replace the cartridge.

- Shower arm
- Collar nut
- Swivel ball nut
- Spray adjustment cam lever
- Swivel ball
- O-ring
- Spray outlets

Fixing & Replacing Shower Heads

If spray from the shower head is uneven, clean the spray holes. The outlet or inlet holes of the shower head may get clogged with mineral deposits.

Shower heads pivot into different positions. If a shower head does not stay in position, or if it leaks, replace the O-ring that seals against the swivel ball.

A tub can be equipped with a shower by installing a flexible shower adapter kit. Complete kits are available at hardware stores and home centers.

A typical shower head can be disassembled easily for cleaning and repair. Some shower heads include a spray adjustment cam lever that is used to change the force of the spray.

Everything You Need:

Tools: adjustable wrench or channel-type pliers, pipe wrench, drill, glass & tile bit (if needed), mallet, screwdriver.

Materials: masking tape, thin wire (paper clip), heatproof grease, rag, replacement O-rings (if needed), masonry anchors, flexible shower adapter kit (optional).

How to Clean & Repair a Shower Head

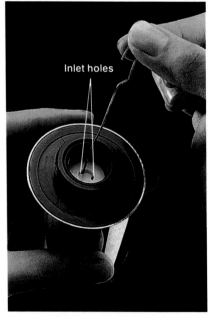

Swivel ball nut

Collar nut

Inlet holes

O-ring

1 Unscrew swivel ball nut, using an adjustable wrench or channel-type pliers. Wrap jaws of the tool with masking tape to prevent marring the finish. Unscrew collar nut from shower head.

2 Clean outlet and inlet holes of shower head with a thin wire. Flush the head with clean water.

3 Replace the O-ring, if necessary. Lubricate the O-ring with heatproof grease before installing.

How to Install a Flexible Shower Adapter

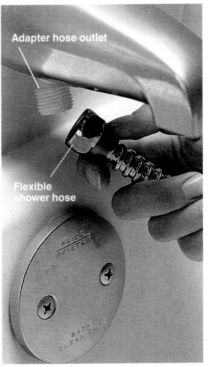

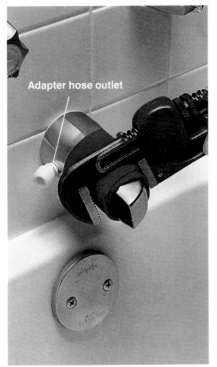

1 Remove old tub spout (page 103). Install new tub spout from kit, using a pipe wrench. New spout will have an adapter hose outlet. Wrap the tub spout with a rag to prevent damage to the chrome finish.

2 Attach flexible shower hose to the adaptor hose outlet. Tighten with an adjustable wrench or channel-type pliers.

3 Determine location of shower head hanger. Use hose length as a guide, and make sure shower head can be easily lifted off hanger.

4 Mark hole locations. Use a glass and tile bit to drill holes in ceramic tile for masonry anchors.

5 Insert anchors into holes, and tap into place with a wooden or rubber mallet.

6 Fasten shower head holder to the wall, and hang shower head.

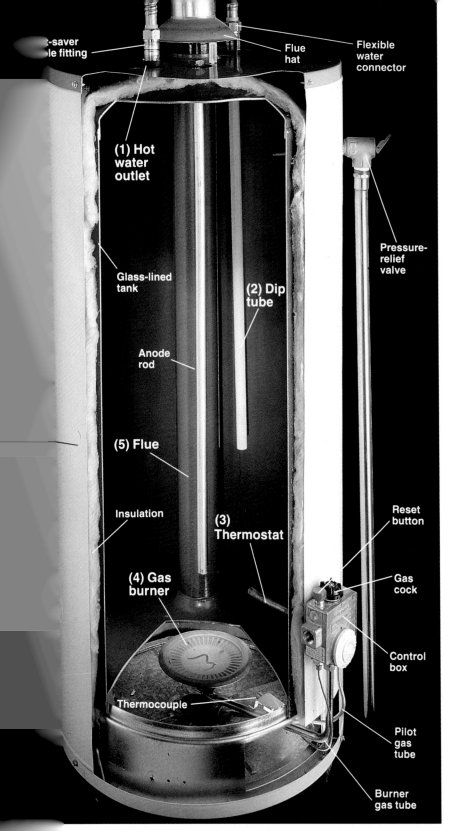

-saver
le fitting

Flue
hat

Flexible
water
connector

**(1) Hot
water
outlet**

Pressure-
relief
valve

**Glass-lined
tank**

**(2) Dip
tube**

Anode
rod

(5) Flue

Reset
button

Insulation

**(3)
Thermostat**

Gas
cock

**(4) Gas
burner**

Control
box

Thermocouple

Pilot
gas
tube

Burner
gas tube

gas water heater works: Hot water leaves tank through the **hot** utlet **(1)** as fresh, cold water enters the water heater through the **(2).** As the water temperature drops, the **thermostat (3)** opens valve, and the **gas burner (4)** is lighted by pilot flame. Exhaust gases ed through **flue (5).** When water temperature reaches preset tem-, the thermostat closes gas valve, extinguishing burner. The thermo-protects against gas leaks by automatically shutting off gas if pilot es out. Anode rod protects tank lining from rust by attracting cor-ements in the water. Pressure-relief valve guards against ruptures by steam buildup in tank.

Fixing a Water Heater

Standard tank water heaters are designed so that repairs are simple. All water heaters have convenient access panels that make it easy to replace worn-out parts. When buying new water heater parts, make sure the replacements match the specifications of your water heater. Most water heaters have a nameplate (page 114) that lists the information needed, including the pressure rating of the tank, and the voltage and wattage ratings of the electric heating elements.

Many water heater problems can be avoided with routine yearly maintenance. Flush the water heater once a year, and test the pressure-relief valve. Set the thermostat at a lower water temperature to prevent heat damage to the tank. (Note: water temperature may affect the efficiency of automatic dishwashers. Check manufacturer's directions for recommended water temperature.) Water heaters last about 10 years on average, but with regular maintenance, a water heater can last 20 years or more.

Do not install an insulating jacket around a gas water heater. Insulation can block air supply and prevent the water heater from ventilating properly. Many water heater manufacturers prohibit the use of insulating jackets. To save energy, insulate the hot water pipes instead, using the materials described on page 122.

The pressure-relief valve is an important safety device that should be checked at least once each year and replaced, if needed. When replacing the pressure-relief valve, shut off the water and drain several gallons of water from the tank.

Problems	Repairs
No hot water, or not enough hot water.	1. **Gas heater**: Make sure gas is on, then relight pilot flame (page 119). **Electric heater:** Make sure power is on, then reset thermostat (page 121). 2. Flush water heater to remove sediment in tank (photo, below). 3. Insulate hot water pipes to reduce heat loss (page 122). 4. **Gas heater:** Clean gas burner & replace thermocouple (pages 110 to 111). **Electric heater**: Replace heating element or thermostat (pages 112 to 113). 5. Raise temperature setting of thermostat.
Pressure-relief valve leaks.	1. Lower the temperature setting (photo, below). 2. Install a new pressure-relief valve (pages 116 to 117, steps 10 to 11).
Pilot flame will not stay lighted.	Clean gas burner & replace the thermocouple (pages 110 to 111).
Water heater leaks around base of tank.	Replace the water heater immediately (pages 114 to 121).

Tips for Maintaining a Water Heater

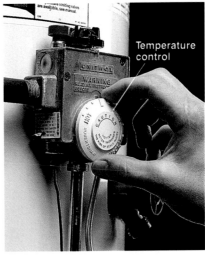

Flush the water heater once a year by draining several gallons of water from the tank. Flushing removes sediment buildup that causes corrosion and reduces heating efficiency.

Test pressure-relief valve once a year. Lift up on lever and let it snap back. Valve should allow a burst of water into drain pipe. If not, install new valve (pages 116 to 117, steps 10 to 11).

Lower the temperature setting on thermostat to 120° F. Lower temperature setting reduces damage to tank caused by overheating, and also reduces energy use.

Fixing a Gas Water Heater

If a gas water heater does not heat water, first remove the outer and inner access panels and make sure the pilot is lighted. To relight a pilot, see steps 20 to 23, page 119. During operation, the outer and inner access panels must be in place. Operating the water heater without the access panels may allow air drafts to blow out the pilot flame.

If the pilot will not light, it is probably because the thermocouple is worn out. The thermocouple is a safety device designed to shut off the gas automatically if the pilot flame goes out. The thermocouple is a thin copper wire that runs from the control box to the gas burner. New thermocouples are inexpensive, and can be installed in a few minutes.

If the gas burner does not light even though the pilot flame is working, or if the gas burns with a yellow, smoky flame, the burner and the pilot gas tube should be cleaned. Clean the burner and gas tube annually to improve energy efficiency and extend the life of the water heater.

A gas water heater must be well ventilated. If you smell smoke or fumes coming from a water heater, shut off the water heater and make sure the exhaust duct is not clogged with soot. A rusted duct must be replaced.

Remember to shut off the gas before beginning work.

Everything You Need:

Tools: adjustable wrench, vacuum cleaner, needlenose pliers.

Materials: thin wire, replacement thermocouple.

How to Clean a Gas Burner & Replace a Thermocouple

1 Shut off gas by turning the gas cock on top of the control box to the OFF position. Wait 10 minutes for gas to dissipate.

2 Disconnect the pilot gas tube, the burner gas tube, and the thermocouple from the bottom of the control box, using an adjustable wrench.

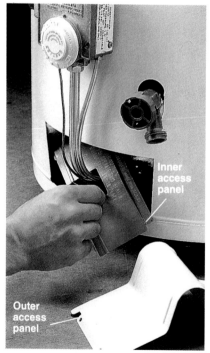

3 Remove the outer and inner access panels covering the burner chamber.

4 Pull down slightly on the pilot gas tube, the burner gas tube, and thermocouple wire to free them from the control box. Tilt the burner unit slightly and remove it from the burner chamber.

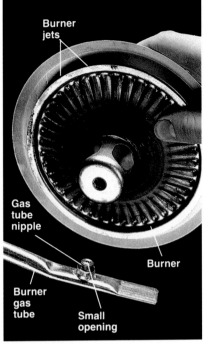

5 Unscrew burner from burner gas tube nipple. Clean small opening in nipple, using a piece of thin wire. Vacuum out burner jets and the burner chamber.

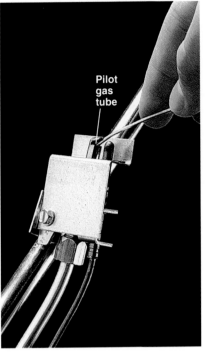

6 Clean the pilot gas tube with a piece of wire. Vacuum out any loose particles. Screw burner onto gas tube nipple.

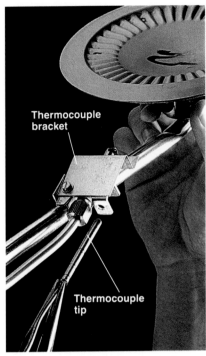

7 Pull the old thermocouple from bracket. Install new thermocouple by pushing the tip into the bracket until it snaps into place.

8 Insert the burner unit into the chamber. Flat tab at end of burner should fit into slotted opening in mounting bracket at the bottom of the chamber.

9 Reconnect the gas tubes and the thermocouple to the control box. Turn on the gas and test for leaks (page 118, step 19). Light the pilot (page 119, steps 20 to 23).

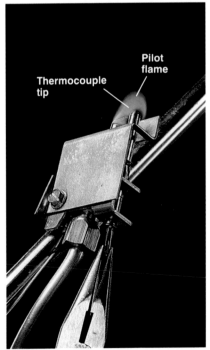

10 Make sure pilot flame wraps around tip of thermocouple. If needed, adjust thermocouple with needlenose pliers until tip is in flame. Replace the inner and outer access panels.

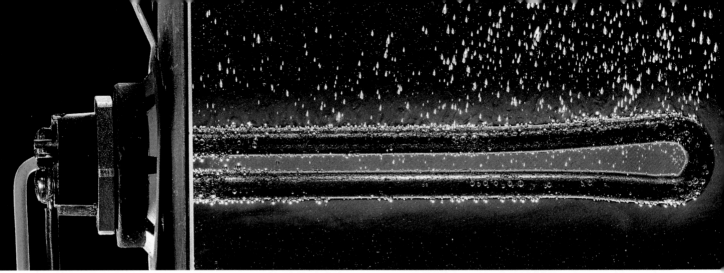

Electric water heater has one or two heating elements mounted in the side wall of the heater. Each element is connected to its own thermostat. When buying a replacement heating element or thermostat, make sure the replacement has same voltage and wattage rating as old part. This information is found on the nameplate (page 114).

Fixing an Electric Water Heater

The most common problem with an electric water heater is a burned-out heating element. Many electric water heaters have two heating elements. To determine which element has failed, turn on a hot water faucet and test the temperature. If the water heater produces water that is warm, but not hot, replace the top heating element. If the heater produces a small amount of very hot water, followed by cold water, replace the bottom heating element.

If replacing the heating element does not solve the problem, then the thermostat may need to be replaced. These parts are found under convenient access panels on the side of the heater.

Remember to turn off the power and test for current before touching wires (page 120, step 4).

Everything You Need:

Tools: screwdriver, gloves, neon circuit tester, channel-type pliers.

Materials: masking tape, replacement heating element or thermostat, replacement gasket, pipe joint compound.

How to Replace an Electric Thermostat

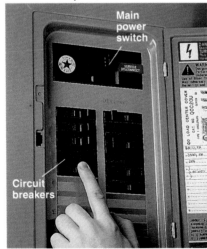

1 Turn off power at main service panel. Remove access panel on side of heater, and **test for current (page 120, step 4).**

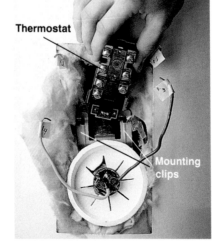

2 Disconnect thermostat wires, and label connections with masking tape. Pull old thermostat out of mounting clips. Snap new thermostat into place, and reconnect wires.

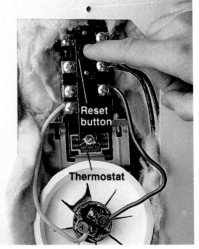

3 Press thermostat reset button, then use a screwdriver to set thermostat to desired temperature. Replace insulation and access panel. Turn on power.

How to Replace an Electric Heating Element

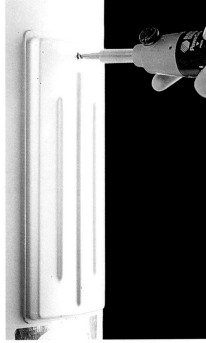

1 Remove access panel on side of water heater. Shut off power to water heater (page 120, step 1). Close the shutoff valves, then drain tank (page 115, step 3).

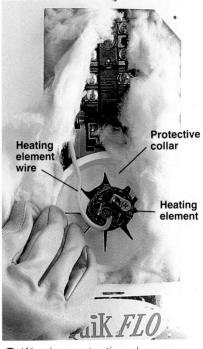

2 Wearing protective gloves, carefully move insulation aside. **Caution: test for current (page 120, step 4)**, then disconnect wires on heating element. Remove protective collar.

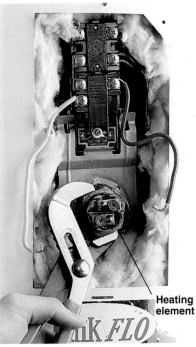

3 Unscrew the heating element with channel-type pliers. Remove old gasket from around water heater opening. Coat both sides of new gasket with pipe joint compound.

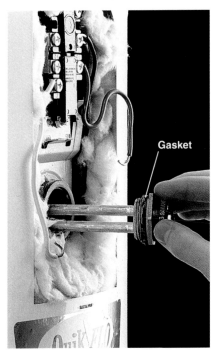

4 Slide new gasket over heating element, and screw element into the tank. Tighten element with channel-type pliers.

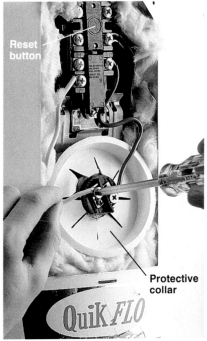

5 Replace protective collar, and reconnect all wires. Turn on hot water faucets throughout house, then turn on water heater shutoff valves. When tap water runs steadily, close faucets.

6 Use a screwdriver to set thermostat to desired temperature. Press thermostat reset buttons. Fold insulation over thermostat, and replace the access panel. Turn on power.

Replacing a Water Heater

A water heater that leaks should be replaced immediately to prevent expensive water damage. Leaks occur because the inner tank has rusted through.

When replacing an electric water heater, make sure the voltage of the new model is the same as the old heater. When replacing a gas water heater, maintain a clearance of 6" or more around the unit for ventilation. Water heaters are available with tank sizes ranging from 30 to 65 gallons. A 40-gallon heater is large enough for a family of four.

Energy-efficient water heaters have polyurethane foam insulation, and usually carry an extended warranty. These models are more expensive, but over the life of the water heater they cost less to own and operate. Some top-quality water heaters have two anode rods for extra corrosion protection.

The pressure-relief valve usually must be purchased separately. Make sure the new valve matches the *working pressure* rating of the tank (photo, left).

Everything You Need:

Tools: pipe wrenches, hacksaw or tubing cutter, screwdriver, hammer, appliance dolly, level, small wire brush, propane torch, adjustable wrench, circuit tester (electric heaters).

Materials: bucket, wood shims, #4 gauge ⅜" sheetmetal screws, pressure-relief valve, threaded male pipe adapters, solder, two heat-saver nipples, Teflon™ tape, flexible water connectors, ¾" copper pipe, pipe joint compound, sponge, masking tape.

Nameplate on side of water heater lists tank capacity, insulation R-value, and working pressure (pounds-per-square-inch). More efficient water heaters have an insulation R-value of 7 or higher. Nameplate for an electric water heater includes the voltage and the wattage capacity of the heating elements and thermostats. Water heaters also have a yellow **energy guide label** (photo, top) that lists typical yearly operating costs. Estimates are based on national averages. Energy costs in your area may differ.

How to Replace a Gas Water Heater

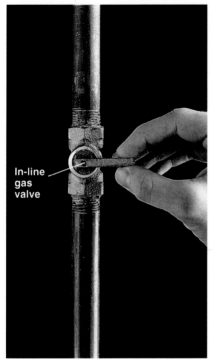

1 Shut off the gas by turning the handle of the in-line valve so it is perpendicular to gas line. Wait 10 minutes for gas to dissipate. Shut off the water supply at the shutoff valves (photo, below).

2 Disconnect gas line at the union fitting or at the flare fitting below shutoff valve, using pipe wrenches. Disassemble and save the gas pipes and fittings.

3 Drain water from the water heater tank by opening the hose bib on the side of the tank. Drain the water into buckets, or attach a hose and empty the tank into a floor drain.

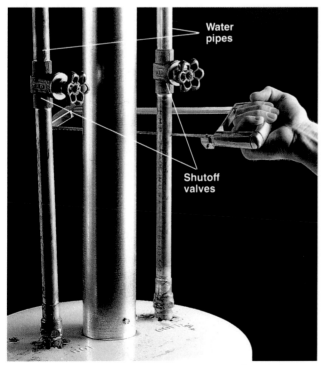

4 Disconnect the hot and cold water pipes above the water heater. If pipes are soldered copper, use a hacksaw or tubing cutter to cut through water pipes just below shutoff valves. Cuts must be straight.

5 Disconnect the exhaust duct by removing the sheetmetal screws. Remove the old water heater with a rented appliance dolly.

(continued next page)

How to Replace a Gas Water Heater (continued)

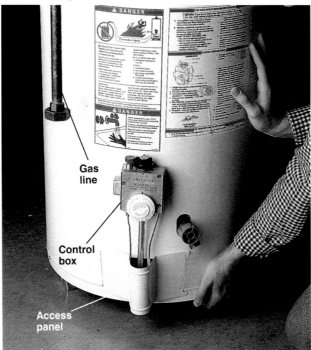

6 Position new heater so that control box is close to gas line, and access panel for burner chamber is not obstructed.

7 Level the water heater by placing wood shims under the legs.

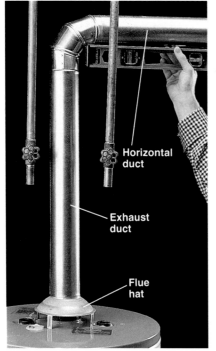

8 Position flue hat so legs fit into slots on water heater, then slip exhaust duct over flue hat. Make sure horizontal duct slopes upward ¼" per foot so fumes cannot back up into house.

9 Attach the flue hat to the exhaust duct with #4 gauge ⅜" sheet-metal screws driven every 4".

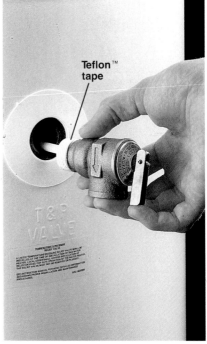

10 Wrap threads of new pressure-relief valve with Teflon™ tape, and screw valve into tank opening with a pipe wrench.

116

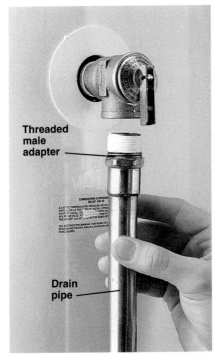

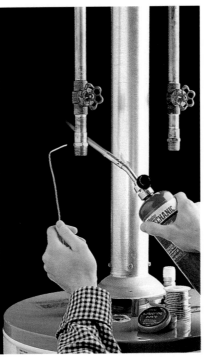

Threaded male adapter

Drain pipe

11 Attach a copper or CPVC drain pipe to the pressure-relief valve, using threaded male adapter (page 17). Pipe should reach to within 3" of floor.

12 Solder threaded male adapters to the water pipes (pages 20 to 25). Let pipes cool, then wrap Teflon™ tape around threads of adapters.

13 Wrap Teflon™ tape around the threads of two heat-saver nipples. The nipples are color-coded, and have water-direction arrows to ensure proper installation.

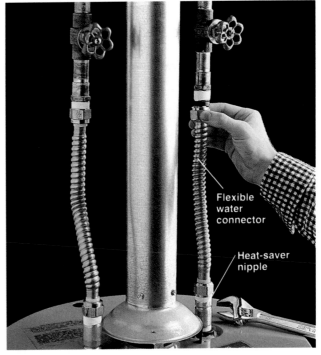

WARNING

Water direction arrow

Cold water inlet

Flexible water connector

Heat-saver nipple

14 Attach blue-coded nipple fitting to cold water inlet and red-coded fitting to hot water outlet, using a pipe wrench. On cold water nipple, water direction arrow should face down; on hot water nipple, arrow should face up.

15 Connect the water lines to the heat-saver nipples with flexible water connectors. Tighten fittings with an adjustable wrench.

(continued next page)

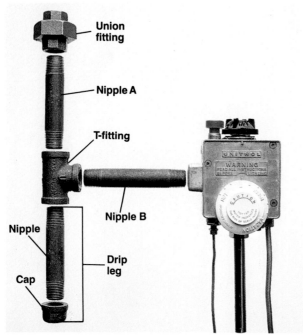

16 Test-fit gas pipes and fittings from old water heater (step 2). One or two new black-iron nipples (A, B) may be necessary if new water heater is taller or shorter than old heater. Use black iron, not galvanized iron, for gas lines. Capped nipple is called a drip leg. The drip leg protects the gas burner by catching dirt particles.

17 Clean pipe threads with a small wire brush, and coat the threads with pipe joint compound. Assemble gas line in the following order: control box nipple (1), T-fitting (2), vertical nipple (3), union fitting (4), vertical nipple (5), cap (6). (Black iron is fitted using same methods as for galvanized iron. See pages 38 to 41 for more information.)

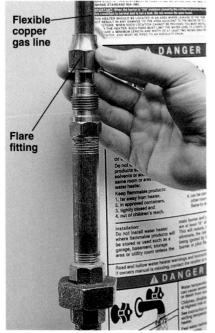

Alternate: If gas line is made of flexible copper, use a flare fitting to connect the gas line to the water heater. (For more information on flare fittings, see pages 28 to 29.)

18 Open the hot water faucets throughout house, then open the water heater inlet and outlet shut-off valves. When water runs steadily from faucets, close faucets.

19 Open the in-line valve on the gas line (step 1). Test for leaks by dabbing soapy water on each joint. Leaking gas will cause water to bubble. Tighten leaking joints with a pipe wrench.

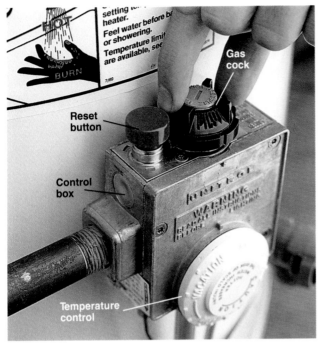

20 Turn the gas cock on top of control box to the PILOT position. Set the temperature control on front of box to desired temperature.

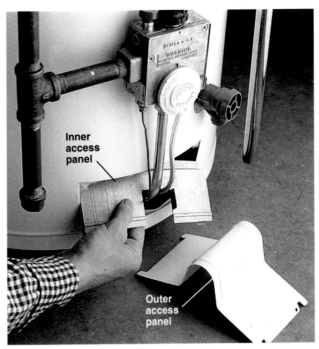

21 Remove the outer and inner access panels covering the burner chamber.

22 Light a match, and hold flame next to the end of the pilot gas tube inside the burner chamber.

23 While holding match next to end of pilot gas tube, press the reset button on top of control box. When pilot flame lights, continue to hold reset button for one minute. Turn gas cock to ON position, and replace the inner and outer access panels.

How to Replace a 220/240-volt Electric Water Heater

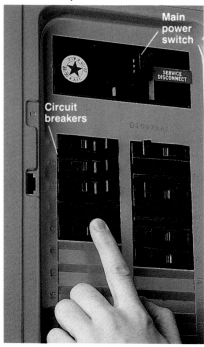

1 Turn off power to water heater by switching off circuit breaker (or removing fuse) at main service panel. Drain water heater and disconnect water pipes (page 115, steps 3 to 4).

2 Remove one of the heating element access panels on the side of the water heater.

3 Wearing protective gloves, fold back the insulation to expose the thermostat. **Caution: do not touch bare wires until they have been tested for current.**

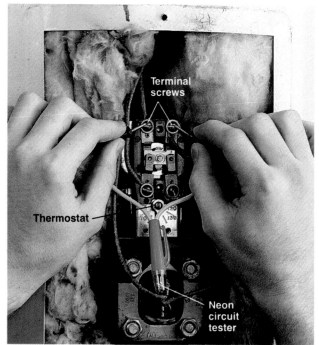

4 Test for current by touching probes of neon circuit tester to top pair of terminal screws on the thermostat. If tester lights, wires are not safe to work on; turn off main power switch and retest for current.

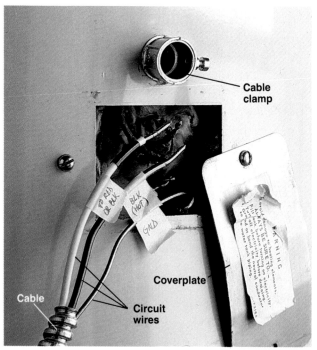

5 Remove coverplate on electrical box, found at side or top of water heater. Disconnect all wires, and label with masking tape for reference. Loosen cable clamp. Remove wires by pulling them through clamp. Remove old heater, then position new heater.

Water pipe

Flexible water connector

6 Connect water pipes and pressure-relief valve, following directions for gas water heaters (pages 116 to 117, steps 10 to 15). Open hot water faucets throughout house, and turn on water. When water runs steadily, turn off faucets.

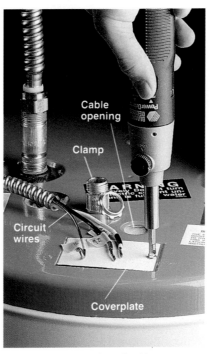

Cable opening

Clamp

Circuit wires

Coverplate

7 Remove the electrical box cover-plate on new water heater. Thread the circuit wires through the clamp. Thread circuit wires through the cable opening on the water heater, and attach clamp to water heater.

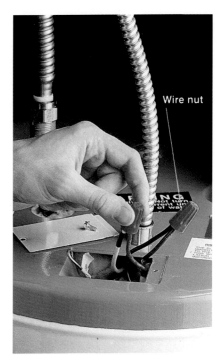

Wire nut

8 Connect the circuit wires to the water heater wires, using wire nuts.

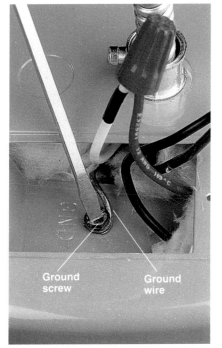

Ground screw

Ground wire

9 Attach bare copper or green ground wire to ground screw. Replace coverplate.

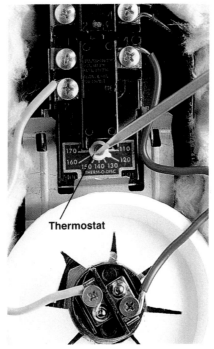

Thermostat

10 Remove access panels on side of water heater (steps 2 to 3), and use a screwdriver to set thermostats to desired water temperature.

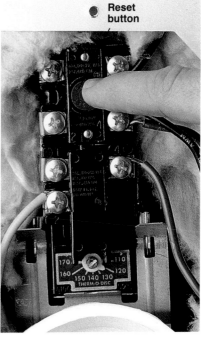

Reset button

11 Press reset button on thermo-stats. Replace the insulation and access panels. Turn on power.

Fixing Burst or Frozen Pipes

When a pipe bursts, immediately turn off the water at the main shutoff valve. Make temporary repairs with a sleeve clamp repair kit (page opposite).

A burst pipe is usually caused by freezing water. Prevent freezes by insulating pipes that run in crawl spaces or other unheated areas.

Pipes that freeze, but do not burst, will block water flow to faucets or appliances. Frozen pipes are easily thawed, but determining the exact location of the blockage may be difficult. Leave blocked faucets or valves turned on. Trace supply pipes that lead to blocked faucet or valve, and look for places where the line runs close to exterior walls or unheated areas. Thaw pipes with a heat gun or hair dryer (below).

Old fittings or corroded pipe also may leak or rupture. Fix old pipes according to the guidelines described on pages 18 to 45.

Everything You Need:

Tools: heat gun or hair dryer, gloves, metal file, screwdriver.

Materials: pipe insulation, sleeve clamp repair kit.

Begin any emergency repair by turning off water supply at main shutoff valve. The main shutoff valve is usually located near water meter.

How to Repair Pipes Blocked with Ice

1 Thaw pipes with a heat gun or hair dryer. Use heat gun on low setting, and keep nozzle moving to prevent overheating pipes.

2 Let pipes cool, then insulate with sleeve-type foam insulation to prevent freezing. Use pipe insulation in crawl spaces or other unheated areas.

Alternate: Insulate pipes with fiberglass strip insulation and waterproof wrap. Wrap insulating strips loosely for best protection.

How to Temporarily Fix a Burst Pipe

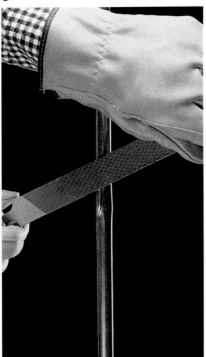

1 Turn off water at main shutoff valve. Heat pipe gently with heat gun or hair dryer. Keep nozzle moving. Once frozen area is thawed, allow pipe to drain.

2 Smooth rough edges of rupture with metal file.

3 Place rubber sleeve of repair clamp around rupture. Make sure seam of sleeve is on opposite side of pipe from rupture.

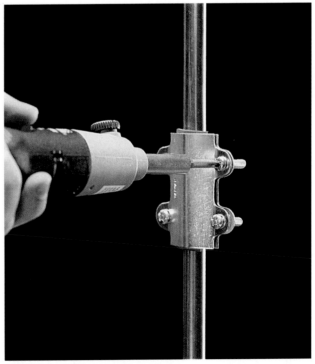

4 Place the two metal repair clamps around rubber sleeve.

5 Tighten screws with screwdriver. Open water supply and watch for leaks. If repair clamp leaks, retighten screws. **Caution: repairs made with a repair clamp kit are temporary.** Replace ruptured section of pipe as soon as possible.

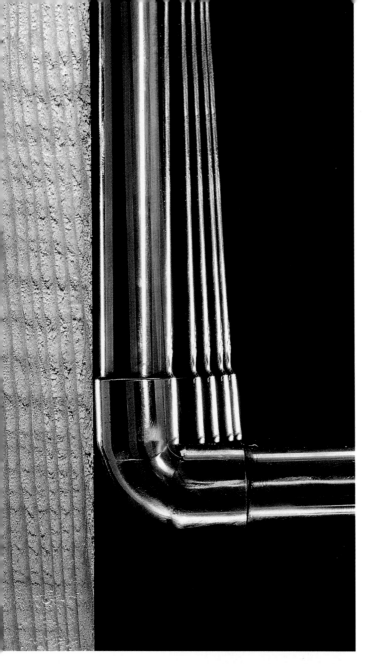

Quieting Noisy Pipes

Pipes can make a loud banging noise when faucets are turned off or when valves on clothes washing machines (or other automatic appliances) shut abruptly. The sudden stop of flowing water creates a shock wave, called water hammer, that slams through the water supply system. Some pipes may knock against wall studs or joists, creating additional noise.

Stop water hammer by installing an air chamber. An air chamber is simply a vertical length of pipe installed in the supply line. An air chamber provides a cushion of air to absorb the shock wave of water hammer. More than one air chamber may be needed to stop water hammer completely.

In time, air in an air chamber may be dissolved by water in the pipes. To restore the air in the chamber, drain the water supply system (page 6). When the system is refilled, the air will be restored.

Pipes that bang against studs or joists can be quieted by cushioning them with pieces of pipe insulation. Make sure pipe hangers are snug and that pipes are well supported.

Everything You Need:

Tools: utility knife, reciprocating saw or hacksaw, propane torch (for sweating copper), pipe wrenches (for galvanized iron).

Materials: foam rubber pipe insulation, pipe and fittings as needed.

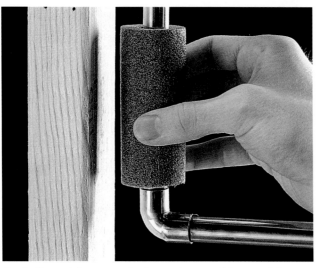

Install cushions made from pieces of foam rubber pipe insulation to prevent pipes from banging against wall studs or joists.

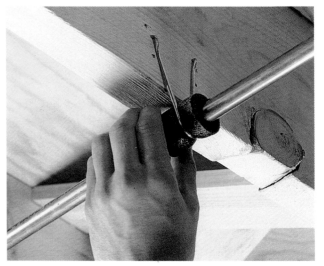

Loose pipes may bang or rub against joist hangers, creating unwanted noises. Use pieces of foam rubber pipe insulation to cushion pipes.

How to Install an Air Chamber

1 Shut off water supply and drain pipes. Measure and cut out a section of horizontal pipe for T-fitting (pages 19 to 21).

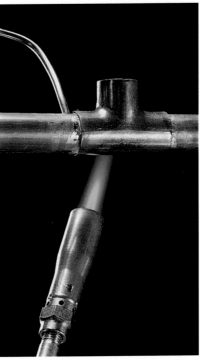

2 Install T-fitting in upright position. Use techniques described in the tools and materials section of this book (pages 10 to 41).

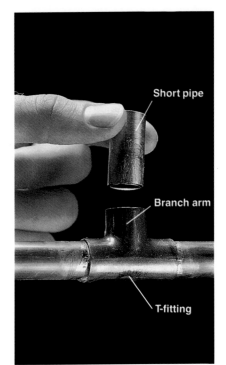

3 Install a short piece of pipe in the branch arm of the T-fitting. This short pipe will be necessary to attach reducer fitting (step 4).

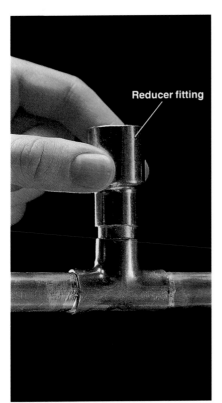

4 Install reducer fitting. Use reducer to make sure diameter of air chamber pipe is larger than supply pipe.

5 Install 12'' long section of pipe for air chamber.

6 Add cap to air chamber. Turn on water supply.

Index